A good, healthy, affirming, "how-to" book which can reduce the risk of sexual abuse for ALL children, with and without disabilities.

Anderson and Paceley have done it again!

What people are saying about
<u>Safe Beginnings:</u>

- How often does one get to hear from survivors of 60+ years ago? Ms. Paceley and Ms. Anderson bring a lifetime of wisdom and maturity to this guidebook. The reader is never able to forget why the authors know so much.
- Full of rich developmental information and practical tips, this book will be surprising to many parents, but the common sense always shows through.

Michael Trout, MA, Director, The Infant-Parent Institute; Founding President, International Association for Infant Mental Health.

- How many times over the years have I heard the expression "Children don't come with a 'how to' book"? Well, this book is just that…covers the full-spectrum from parenting, to teachers, to finding a caregiver, to abusers, to children growing up. WOW! Thanks on behalf of all the parents and children who will benefit from your expertise.
- I wish I would have had a book like this as a young mother. A book like this would have taken a lot of the 'fear and uncertainty' out of being a mother.

Peg Kovach, Executive Director, Growing Strong Sexual Assault Center.

- I especially liked the section dedicated to day care providers which went into detail regarding privacy and expression of feelings.
- I will definitely have to purchase this book for my personal collection to use as a reference and to educate others!!

French Wilson, parent, Human Relations and Training Officer.

- A valuable resource for all parents and day care providers - it's prevention made easy!!
- An essential tool for every parent - this straightforward, easy to read prevention book provides absolutely essential information. The set of skills are written with examples of what to say and why.

Susan Madison, trainer.

- One of the few books that offers concrete suggestions that will empower children to avoid sexual predators.

Pamela Herendeen, RN, MS, Pediatric Nurse Practitioner; Medical Provider of REACH, Referral Evaluation of Abused Children, at Golisano Children's Hospital; National Association of Pediatric Associates and Practitioners, Co-Chairperson of Child Maltreatment Special Interest Group.

- Thank you for providing us this information for our special population, guardians, caregivers and society at large.
- I have already used some of these techniques with my son who is mentally impaired and he has accepted them in a positive manner.

Rosie Kuhlman, parent.

- A fantastic resource! A great yet easy to understand entry to providing realistic information to parents, educators, and caregivers, Great work!

Krista Flores, Project Access Manager
California Coalition Against Sexual Assault

SAFE BEGINNINGS

Protecting Our Children From Sexual Abuse

SAFE BEGINNINGS

PROTECTING OUR CHILDREN
FROM SEXUAL ABUSE

By: Orieda Horn Anderson
and
Shirley Paceley

Blue Tower Training Center

2003

Safe Beginnings
Protecting Our Children From Sexual Abuse
Orieda Horn-Anderson and Shirley Paceley

BLUE TOWER TRAINING CENTER
A division of Macon Resources, Inc.
P.O. Box 2760
Decatur, IL. 62524-2760

Children illustrations by Crist Cruz
Cover design by Scott Hawbaker and Crist Cruz
Typesetting and Layout by Sherry Ridley
ISBN: 1-931568-20-0

Library of Congress Control Number
2003103865

Printed in the U.S.A.

Dedicated to Orien and Eda Garner Horn who shared their protoplasm to create me with my uniqueness, and by sharing their names to create the unique name Orieda. I love you with a never-ending love.

Your daughter, Orieda

Dedicated to Megan, whose spirit and strength inspires me daily to continue to fight for equality and justice.

Shirley

The female pronoun used in this book refers to both genders.

Table Of Contents

Acknowledgments

We sincerely appreciate the support and assistance of the many people who contributed to the creation of this work. Before our first prevention book was even published, Kay Scrogin suggested that we consider writing a second sexual abuse prevention book which included ALL preschool children. And now, thanks to the following people, that idea is a reality; Karen Randolph, Leslie Pearce, Linda Allen-Smith, French Wilson, Debbie Schmiederjan, Tammy Bennett, Jean Moore (Macon County Child Advocacy Center) and Peg Kovach (Growing Strong Sexual Assault Center) all contributed their thoughts and ideas to the initial draft of <u>Safe Beginnings</u>. Deanna Hammond created the two illustrations in the Creating Safe Environments section and Crist Cruz volunteered his time and talent creating the children faces you see throughout the book. We appreciate the parents and professionals who reviewed the manuscript and offered their comments, including Winifred Kempton, Michael Trout, Susan Madison, Dr. Sol Gordon, Rosie Kuhlman, Krista Flores, and Pam Herendeen. Elizabeth McGlade provided clerical support for mailings and Linda Clary provided overall clerical and computer assistance. Sherry Ridley brought it all together and actually made it look like a book and Scott Hawbaker designed the book cover from a concept developed by Crist Cruz. We appreciate each of your contributions.

We also want to thank Orieda's daughter, Judith Franing, and her husband, Howard, and Shirley's beloved Crist, for their ongoing support of our work together. We especially want to thank the many people who have survived sexual abuse and allowed us to be a part of their lives. Because of you, we know that there is amazing strength in the human spirit and always hope for recovery.

Orieda and Shirley

Introduction

Light tomorrow with today.
                                    Elizabeth Barrett Browing

A personal note from Shirley

I was sexually abused beginning at age two or three and continuing for several years. It would be a few decades later before I was able to acknowledge and begin to understand what had happened to me and how it had affected my life. I often wonder what could have changed my early childhood experiences. When I review sexual abuse prevention programs, I ask myself two personal questions: "Would this program have kept me safe from abuse?" and "Would I have been able to tell someone earlier?" I know that as long as there are sex offenders in the world, there will be victims of sexual abuse. I also know that the sooner sexual abuse is reported, the less damage there is for the victim. I also believe that if we start early in a child's life, we can develop a healthy, happy, empowered child who is more likely to resist and report abuse. That is what this book is all about...**safe beginnings**!

On my bulletin board lives a button that reads, ALLOW FOR THE POSSIBILITY.
- It pushes me to never give up.
- It reminds me that all people can learn.
- When I cry for another victim, it gently gives me hope.

As you read this book:
- Allow for the possibility that you can make a difference by teaching your child these skills.
- Allow for the possibility that you can create safer environments in homes, day care centers and schools.
- Allow for the possibility that we can raise boys who will become men who will not harm others.
- Allow for the possibility that we can change the world, one person at a time, and that you are the hope for a safe future.

A personal note from Orieda

My family experienced two earth-shattering experiences within a two month time period. My youngest sister, who in her innocence said, "I was third the three of October" told our mother that our elderly next door neighbor "put his fingers in my pee-pee". Our father called the family doctor, related what had happened and asked what he should do. Dr. Johnson said, "Get a two by four and beat his brains out". Of course, dad did not physically attack the elderly man but he had a strong verbal confrontation with him. The man and his family moved from the neighborhood within the week.

Two months later, shortly after my ninth birthday, one Saturday my paternal grandfather and I were left alone. He cornered me in the upstairs playroom, threw me on the bed, ripped off my bloomers and proceeded to rape me. I was fighting like a 'trapped tiger'. I broke loose when I heard my father's car door slam shut. I screamed at Granddad "I'm going to tell daddy what you have done!" Granddad said, "This is our secret. You tell him and I'll kill you the next time I get my hands on you." I screamed, "I can run faster than you can" and ran to my dad and told him. He threw his arms around me, held me safely in his arms repeating "I'm so sorry. I'm so sorry. He will never do this to another child." And he didn't. The following Monday, after dad made arrangements to have his father admitted to a mental institution in granddad's home state, he put his father in the car for the trip. In route, granddad contracted pneumonia and died.

I now know I was not his only victim. Other granddaughters were abused by him and told no one. Recently, after 70 plus years of keeping "his secret", they have shared their sexual abuse with me. There were other young victims, some of whom were my playmates. My grandfather was a pedophile.

After the molestation of my youngest sister and my parents response to her, it affirmed my trust that I could safely tell them and they would believe me. These two incidents were openly discussed with us. We were instructed, "If anyone touches your private parts we need to be told. These are not secrets you keep. Remember this was not your fault. Do not feel guilty."

I believed that after the rape I was still a virgin. I was taught that virginity was shared when two people gave themselves to one another in intimacy and love. Virginity is not an intact hymen. Virginity for both genders is not stolen if rape, molestation or sexual abuse occurs.

What did I learn from these experiences?

1. My parents believed and trusted me and I believed and trusted them.
2. These bad experiences were not family "secrets" to be kept secret.
3. That I did not have to carry the rape as a "scarlet letter" or carry it as a millstone around my neck. It was a dreadful experience but did not need to be a forever nightmare.
4. To quote William Faulkner, "The past is never dead. It is never even past." The past is part of who I am today and while I can learn from it, it will always be a part of me.

The vividness in which I remember the rape seventy plus years is evident that the "Past is never dead. It is never even past". I remember the pinstripes on his dark pants, the bone colored buttons on his pants, the urine-stained BVDs underwear, him holding me down with one arm and holding his erect penis with the other hand as he thrust his body between my legs. The immediate support, comfort and understanding by my parents contrasts the difference in the abuse and the effects that Shirley suffered. My abuse was dealt with immediately. Shirley's abuse was over a period of years, and its effect was left to fester as a "cancerous wound" for many years. Through this experience I became a good listener and a sexual abuse counselor beginning in my teen years. I've heard it all. Shirley and I have a similar mission. We are mandated to be instrumental in making changes so that sexual abuse becomes as extinct as the dinosaur.

Sexual abuse can be likened to dropping a huge boulder into a deep body of water. The first sexual abuse encounter to our psyche is like the fierce impact of the boulder hitting the water. Later abusive experiences are like the wake that follows the impacting event. The more frequent the abuses, the less noticeable the wake. There is a numbing effect, leaving the victim with a subconscious feeling of worthlessness, and it becomes a way of life. I remember two brothers, age five and seven who were sexually abused almost daily. The older of the two hesitated to return home after school. He suggested to the younger brother that they should run away. The younger brother said, "Heck no. Let's go in and get it over with so we can go out and play."

If left untreated, the effects can radiate into all areas of one's life and even effect succeeding generations. The mission of this book is to reduce the risks of sexual abuse through education and healthy information. If abuse does occur, truth, knowledge and awareness can provide a protective cover and reduce the lifetime impact.

A Note to Parents

If you have a baby or a young child, you have many important responsibilities. You might be asking: Who/what do I want my child to become? How am I providing for the safety of my child? How can I prepare my child to get along with others? How will my child do in school? Being a parent is a HUGE responsibility!

There are so many precautions we take with our new babies. We support their necks when they are tiny, use car seats, make sure they get their immunizations, give them toys safe for their ages, and numerous other actions. Most parents could make a really long list of tips to keep children safe from illnesses and accidents. But when we ask parents, "What can you do to keep your child safe from sexual abuse?" some say, "I make sure she is always with safe people. That's how I protect her." Many deny the risk and say "It won't happen to **my** child."

This kind of denial is common because for most people it is only something we read about in the paper or hear about on TV. Yet, we all know people who have been affected by sexual abuse. Usually it is kept a secret. Sexual abuse is very common. Men sexually assault girls and women at alarming rates but because of the shame involved, many people who have been sexually abused do not disclose what has happened to them. The shame should be with the man who abuses, not with the victim. There ARE women who sexually abuse children too, but the percent is small…around one percent…but to the victims, the effects are very real.

All too often, following abuse, we have heard a mom or a dad say, "I never thought it could happen in my family. Now I know it can happen to anyone." Denying the possibility of sexual abuse may be more comfortable than facing it. However, when you acknowledge the possibility of sexual abuse, you can equip yourself and your child with tools for prevention.

We know that you don't want to think about or deal with sexuality issues and certainly not sexual abuse. We also know that if your child is sexually abused, the pain and hurt you will experience will be immense. We recognize that you already have an overwhelming amount of issues and concern for your child but we believe education on the prevention of sexual abuse can become part of your daily routine. It is not a hard thing to do and the benefit is life long. We urge you to pay attention. If you have decided to read this book, pat yourself on the back. You are a very busy person yet you have made an important decision for your child's future. We applaud you!!

Please know that we are passionately convinced that the skills in this book can help your child as he or she grows up. We know that it may not be easy to teach some of these skills and you will not always do it perfectly. We are all human and parenting is hard work. So don't be too hard on yourself when you forget to follow one of the guidelines described. Just be as consistent as you can. You are learning along with your child.

There are many advantages to teaching these skills while your child is young. For one thing, your child can learn these skills easier when she is little. You can help your child learn valuable patterns of behavior. When we teach these skills to teenagers or adults, we have to teach them to stop an established pattern before they can learn these new skills. This is really hard and can take a long time. We sometimes teach these skills AFTER a person has been abused or after a 'sexual incident'. We believe that if the skills are taught to young children, we may be able to avoid such problems. Believe it or not, you can actually start teaching your child about healthy sexuality and abuse prevention while she is still a baby!

We know that you do not want your child to be harmed in any way. Prevention of sexual abuse is the goal of this book. If your child is abused, no matter what you have taught her, please know it is not your fault, nor is it your child's fault. Abuse is the fault of the person who commits the act.

A Note to All Who Support Children

This book is for anyone who knows and loves a child who has not yet started school. The information presented comes from many years of working with people who have been sexually abused, and/or who are struggling with sexuality issues.

This book is the result of the pain, anger and frustration we have felt in working with yet another victim…and a result of each victim's pain and anger. Experts indicate that 1 in 3 girls and 1 in 5 boys are sexually assaulted by the time they reach the age of 18. For persons with disabilities, the incidence is even higher. Some experts say as many as 67%, and others say over 90%, of persons with developmental disabilities are sexually abused at some point in their life. *The majority of the people who commit sex offenses are people who are known to, and trusted by, the child. Sex offenses by strangers are less likely to happen than sex offenses by relatives, neighbors, care providers and acquaintances.* This kind of abuse of power against our children is unacceptable and needs to stop! We believe that part of the solution lies with the parents, professionals and others who care about children.

There are many factors which come together when sexual abuse occurs. Some of the factors we have no control over. For example, we do not have control over the person who chooses to abuse someone. However, we do have control over the boundaries and skills we teach our children as well as the environments in which our children spend their time. This book is focused on the factors that we can control, or at least impact, in some way. We will teach you about factors that you have power to control or modify. There is an incredible wealth of knowledge about early childhood development and about prevention of sexual abuse. We have tried to combine this knowledge to give you the skills necessary to nurture your child into a happy, healthy person. The information is designed for preschool children, but the skills described need to be developed/reinforced throughout childhood and adolescence.

We have included a section on creating safe environments in group settings. These settings include child care centers, preschools, church nurseries, group developmental therapy services, special education classes, recreational classes and any group setting for preschool children. It is not enough to teach prevention skills to children. We must create environments which model, train, allow and reinforce those skills. We must create environments which do not attract offenders but repel them. Please read this section with an open mind. At first it may seem like too much work to adopt these practices into your already busy schedule, but we have found that with a little practice, the ideas in this book can be incorporated into your daily life and become routine. The children in your care are worth it!!

This book is a work in progress. It is the product of many tears for the many survivors who have touched our lives and taught us some lessons to pass on to you. It is a product of our hopes and dreams for a safe and healthy future for our children. We welcome your comments, questions and suggestions. We encourage you to develop materials, challenge procedures, fight for prevention programs at schools, and write a better book. It will take all of us to solve the problem of sexual abuse. We welcome you as partners in the struggle.

Orieda and Shirley

SECTION 1

DEFINING HUMAN SEXUALITY

Children should be the first to benefit from the successes of
mankind, and the last to suffer from its failures.

James Grant

Each day of our lives we make deposits
in the memory banks of our children.

Charles Swindell

DEFINING HUMAN SEXUALITY

The following definitions are used within the context of this book.

- Sex: refers to gender...male or female
- Sexual: refers to sexual feelings, activity, and intimacy with self or another.
- Sexuality: refers to all aspects of the person, including physical, emotional, sexual, intellectual and psychological.

Just what do we mean when we talk about human sexuality? First of all, human sexuality is a birthright. Human beings have a right to be sexual...no government, no agency, no illness, no injury, no disability, no parent, and no person has the right to remove our sexuality from us. Secondly, human sexuality is much more than body parts and sexual activity. Human sexuality includes our self-concept, our gender (male or female), our communication style, our feelings, our body, and our relationships. We cannot talk about sexual abuse prevention without talking about healthy sexuality. How do we help our children develop a healthy self-concept and healthy sexuality? Let's start at the beginning.

Your own attitude toward your sexuality will greatly influence the future sexuality of your child. There is a personal survey following this section - A Look Inside Ourselves. Please take time to answer the questions for yourself. Consider your own history and how it has affected your life. If you were a victim of sexual abuse as a child and have not received support and counseling, it is important that you have support to work through your issues related to the abuse. This is important not only for you, but also for your child. Child sexual abuse tends to occur across generations of families. In other words, if you were abused as a child, the chances increase that one of your children may be sexually abused. It is common for a parent to disclose their own abuse after their child has been abused. We encourage you to get help now if you haven't. If you were a sexual abuse victim, you can take steps to break the cycle within your own family. The only way to do this is to acknowledge the abuse, work through your feelings, acknowledge how the abuse has affected you and make changes so that you are healthier in your responses to life.

Your attitude about your pregnancy and the circumstances that surround the conception of your child form the foundation of how you feel about your child. When sexual intimacy occurs between two consenting people of the opposite sex, the partners are consenting to the possibility that a baby might be formed. This is a tremendous responsibility! The moment pregnancy is discovered, your energy should be directed to the new life that is developing. You have created a new generation, with your history…and the immortality of your life has begun by passing your own protoplasm to the next generation.

Your relationship with your baby actually begins during pregnancy. You communicate with the baby through your own attitude. How does the baby know your attitude? You communicate your attitude through your tone of voice, the stress you carry in your body, the touching of your abdomen, etc. The baby hears your voice and the surrounding sounds as her brain develops. Gentle caressing of your abdomen is an important way to communicate your love for and to your baby before you even see her. Talking softly to your baby before birth is a wonderful way to start forming the bond of love and it can be fun too! Memory begins during the fourth month of fetal development so do what you can to make them good memories. You have the opportunity to teach your child about giving and receiving love before she is even born. That is the core of a healthy self-concept.

When your baby is born, the relationship between the two of you continues to grow. In some cases, a parent and child may 'clash' before they even get to know each other. A nervous parent and a cranky baby can make for a strained parent-child relationship. Some people can handle babies who cry a lot with ease…for others, it is a real challenge. And to some extent, this may depend on the amount of support you have. Dealing with a crying baby over days or weeks or months, without any help, can be a strain on the calmest of nerves!! It is okay to ask for and accept help. Parenthood is a full-time job - 24 hours a day…7 days a week…so ask for help when you can and accept it graciously when it is offered. A good parent takes breaks from parenting. It really is okay!! No matter how 'easy' or difficult your baby is to take care of…no matter how healthy or unhealthy your baby is…you have a baby who needs your love and attention. Your attitude towards your baby helps build the foundation for her self-esteem. What you say about your child as well as your body language, in your child's presence is the beginning of how your child will feel about herself. We encourage you to appreciate your child and look for the beauty and unique qualities in her.

> *The mother of a baby girl with severe disabilities once told me: "When I am down, I go to my daughter's crib and speak to her. Her constant smile makes me realize her smile is the sunshine of my life. She accepts me just the way I am, displaying a total love. She is love."*

This is true for all babies. In the beginning they give total acceptance but quickly learn to sort out what they can and cannot trust.

My child is so little, why are we talking about sexuality? Because you are laying the foundation for the development of your child RIGHT NOW. One third of your child's brain development occurs during the first 12 months of life. Eighty per cent of your child's brain development occurs by the time your child reaches the age of three. Your child is learning faster right now than at any time in her life. What you do right now really matters and will affect your child the rest of her life. Why not start right now to develop a healthy, happy and safe child?

Through our personal and professional experiences with many people who have been sexually abused, we have identified some important factors in the prevention of sexual abuse. We will begin by discussing specific skills that you can teach your child which will make her safer. We will review strategies for strengthening these skills beyond the preschool years. A special section will be devoted to creating safe environments, especially in day care settings as well as church nurseries and communal babysitting. We have included some ideas for social changes which we believe can reduce the overall incidence of sexual abuse as well as resources which are available for education and prevention. And, finally, we review information about abusers, signs of abuse and what to do if your child is abused. We believe that information is power. We hope that this information empowers you to make healthy choices for yourself and your children.

A LOOK INSIDE OURSELVES

Please take the time to review the personal history survey. YOU ARE WORTH IT!! Your answers to this survey are personal and private and no one else need know your responses. You choose what you share and with whom.

1. **Were you a child born from love?** Think about your own conception. This may not be something you have ever thought about (and you may not want to think about it...your parent having sex...UUHHH!!) Was your birth planned? What was your parents' relationship like when you were conceived? Your perception of your conception may be related to your perception of yourself.

2. **Did your mother take care of you as a child?** Did your mother provide most of your care when you were an infant...toddler...child? What was her attitude toward you? Were your needs responded to with love? Were you thought of as a nuisance?

3. **Did your father live in the home?** If not, did you have contact with your father on a regular basis? How was your relationship with your father? How did your father view you as a child?

4. **Did you have grandparents, aunts, uncles, siblings that helped take care of you?** Who did you spend a lot of time with? How was your relationship with your grandparents? How did the other primary people in your life feel about you?

5. **Did you have special names for your private parts?** What messages were you given about your genitalia? Were you given slang terms to use for urinate, vulva, penis, etc.? Were these topics ignored?

6. **Did you learn the names penis and vagina before you were a teenager?** Were your caregivers open about sexual terms or did they avoid such topics? How did you learn about menstruation? At what age did you discover gender differences (e.g., playing doctor)?

7. **How did you learn the facts about sexual activity?** Where were you before you were born? Did your parents talk openly with you about sexual intercourse? Where babies come from? Pregnancy? Sexually- transmitted diseases? Wet Dreams? Sexual activity?

8. **Who told you what to do on your first date?** What were you told to do or not do? Did you have a trust person you could talk to about your concerns?

9. **Were you sexually abused as a child?** If yes, was this a single incident or an ongoing situation? Have you told anyone about the abuse, if so, when? Have you received counseling related to the abuse?

10. **What feelings of loss and abandonment did you experience as a child?** What disappointments do you remember? Did you experience a loss due to divorce, extended illness, death of a family member, or loss of a favorite pet? Did you lose a close friend due to a family move?

11. **What feelings of joy, comfort and value did you experience as a child?** What are some of the experiences that made you laugh or smile? What did you do that was valued and appreciated by your family, teachers, neighbors or other adults?

Your answers to these questions are an important part of who you are. Every single person on Earth will have different responses and yet we also have similarities. Look at your answers...listen to them...feel them...embrace them. Celebrate your blessings! If you have discovered any pockets of pain which need to be emptied, make that commitment to yourself by seeking counseling or therapy. You will be a better parent if you do.

SKILLS TO TEACH YOUR CHILD

Children may close their ears to our advice, but open their
eyes to example.

Unknown

SKILLS TO TEACH YOUR CHILD

There are some very specific skills which you can teach your child which can help them to develop a healthy self-concept and help protect them from sexual abuse. These skills include:

- ❖ Identify and express feelings
- ❖ Say "No"
- ❖ Know language for body parts
- ❖ Understand healthy and unhealthy touch
- ❖ Make choices regarding touch
- ❖ Understand social distance
- ❖ Understand different relationships
- ❖ Understand private vs public

Each of these skills is important and can be taught to your child. We need to start early and remember that children learn by what they live. Our children learn best when our words and our actions are consistent. The old saying, "Do what I say and not what I do" does not make for good teaching.

LISTENING IS TEACHING

We all need at least one person in our life who listens to us. Listening is much more than hearing. It is paying close attention to the body language, feelings, spoken word, eye movements, facial expressions, change in appearance, change in skin tone, and body movements, among other things. When we observe these signs of expression from our child and respond in some way that communicates that we are paying attention and trying to understand, we are listening.

When we listen to our children, we in essence are telling them, "What you have to say is important." We are giving them power within the family and we all need to feel that we have some power. When a child is raised in a family with no positive power, the child may learn to 'take power' from others by being 'bad' or using aggression or the child may become helpless and passive and let others 'run over her'. Help your child find a positive place within your family structure. Listening is one way to do that.

Everyone communicates. We each have our own style of communicating. No matter what style of communicating your child has, she needs you to notice and respond. If you are sensitive to your child's means of communication, you will know your child better than anyone and can assure that her needs are met. If you notice a significant change in your child's behavior, think back to what the child has experienced prior to the change and try to figure out the reason for the change. You might even want to write this information down and date it for future reference. Sometimes a change in behavior is due to a physical cause such as a headache or stomach pain. You will learn to become sensitive to these changes and what these changes might mean for your child.

When your child is a toddler, you might want to develop a special bedtime routine which is good for you and for your child. When your child is in bed, discuss the good things that happened that day. Ask your child to tell you some good things that happened during the day. You can add to the list and let your child know that you are happy with her. Some parents even record them in a journal for the child. You can give the 'book' a title if you want. Use your creativity and the creativity of your child to expand on this idea. Bedtime is a wonderful time to 'chat'. We need to spend time everyday talking with our children about 'unimportant' things so that we are able to talk with them about important things when we need to.

If your child is nonverbal, express to your child three things that you noticed during the day. For example, "Today when you got up, you had a beautiful smile and it made me feel so good! I was happy today when you closed the bathroom door. I noticed at dinner, you got your spoon in the bowl so good. I am proud of you." This evening routine is a great way to build your child's self-confidence and a wonderful time for listening and sharing.

When you listen to your child, there is an opportunity for you to learn who your child really is. Teach your child that she is valuable in her own right. She does not have to compete with the next door neighbors or the children on TV. Children are more vulnerable to sexual abuse if they are trying to please someone else, or be like someone else. When we focus on trying to make a child be like someone else, the message to the child is, "You're not good enough". That is a destructive message to the child's self esteem. It is the internal character of the child that counts. Sometimes we over program our children because we want them to shine. We push, push and push them to be more and different. Slow down and be sensitive to each child's needs, preferences, rhythms, and personality. Let your child know she is valued just for who she is. These early years create the foundation.

When you listen to your child, trust develops between the two of you. Listening to your child establishes a rapport between the two of you which makes teaching easier. Listening to your child on a regular basis keeps you in touch with your child and if something does happen to your child, you will be more likely to help your child talk about what happened. Listening to your child allows you to teach the following skills in a more effective way.

FEELINGS

In order to develop a healthy self-concept, a child must have a safe place to identify and express her feelings. You are the provider of that safe place. You do this by accepting and acknowledging the four basic feelings of happy, sad, scared and angry. As your child grows older, you can begin to teach your child to identify and express more complex feelings such as frustration, pride, confusion and embarrassment.
Here are some ways that you can teach your child to identify and express her feelings:

❖ When your child cries, help her learn to label the feeling. You might say, "Oh, you sound mad" if that is the feeling you think the child is trying to express. When your child express any feeling, help your child learn the word that matches her feeling.

❖ It is important that we acknowledge that all feelings are okay. If your child strikes out when angry, you might say, "It is okay to feel mad, but we don't hurt people."

❖ When (if) your child has verbal language, teach your child to say her feelings. For example, you might say, "You look really happy. Can you say 'happy'?" If your child has no spoken language, cut out pictures and see if your child can learn to point to the facial expressions. If your child can express 'yes' and 'no' By shaking her head, signing or pointing to a symbol, ask your child, "Does that make you happy?" and Similar questions throughout the day. Teach your child to respond by using the method she can do (shake head, sign, point).

❖ As you read your child books, ask questions like, "Is this little boy sad?" or "How do you think the dad feels?"

❖ Another way to teach your child is by making a game out of faces; i.e., "Let me see your scared face…Let me see your happy face"...

❖ Remember that all feelings are okay so when your child expresses an intense feeling, acknowledge it. Do not say, "Don't be angry" or "You shouldn't be mad at your sister". The 'feeling' is valid, help your child learn healthy ways to express her hurt or anger. If your child is mad at you and screams "I hate you!", try not to overact. You might respond with "You are really mad at me right now." If a child displays her anger in an aggressive way let your child know that you love her but do not like her behavior."

❖ Another excellent way to teach your child to identify and express her feelings is to identify and express your feelings. For example, "I am happy that you drew me a picture" or "I am sad that grandma is sick". Children learn from our example.

As stated before, all feelings are okay. However, it is important to help your child learn healthy ways to express the feelings that she finds uncomfortable. This can prevent behavior problems in the future. It is equally important to teach your child to express happy feelings. There are many healthy ways your child might learn to express her feelings. Teach and encourage the ones below so your child can find ones that work for her.

❖ Talking about her feelings ❖ Crying
❖ Signing her feelings ❖ Drawing her feelings
❖ Smiling ❖ Taking a walk
❖ Singing ❖ Dancing
❖ Exercising ❖ Petting an animal
❖ Pointing to pictures that express feelings

It is necessary for us to keep our cool when the child gets angry (and they all do). As long as the child is not hurting someone, including herself, or destroying property, she has the right to express her feelings, including anger. What can a parent learn from a child's anger? Often, we can learn the cause of the anger…unwanted touch could be a cause. Use the anger to teach yourself more about your child. The better you know your child, the better you can help her learn safety skills. We should also note that over the years we have worked with a few cases when unwanted touch did not cause anger or fear. When this occurs, we need to teach the person about their rights and how to react to this personal intrusion.

If you help your child to label her feelings when she is little, she will be more likely to express her feelings as she grows. As your child grows older, try and teach her the simple relaxation technique of slow, deep breaths. Many children with learning disabilities or developmental disabilities can also learn this technique. It is also helpful for parents and other caretakers to learn to 'breathe' when they are stressed!! Teach your child that it is hard to solve problems when she is upset.

When your child has an acceptable way to express her feelings, she won't have to keep them inside, nor will she have to explode when they overwhelm her. Many adults that have not learned to accept their pain and manage their emotions have developed destructive habits to cope with uncomfortable emotions. We may 'self-medicate' our pain with food, alcohol, drugs, or violence and not even know that is what we are doing. Teaching your child to express her feelings may be one of the best gifts you will ever give her.

One mother reported that she got very angry and hit her young son with undue force for a small problem. She immediately apologized and told her son that it was actually his grandmother that she was angry with. The son said, "Oh, I see, grandma is too big to hit."

When the children were young, we had a large pantry in the basement. I was preparing lunch one day and needed a can of soup. I asked Ed, "Would you please go down and get me a can of soup for lunch?" Ed replied with "No." I stopped what I was doing and went over to Ed. I bent down and said, "How do we resolve this?" Ed replied, "Let's both go. I'll get the can of soup and you keep the wild animals off of me." My child was not being obstinate, he was afraid.

SAYING "NO"

No we are not kidding!! We all know that most two year olds are quite capable of saying 'No'. Many parents and child care providers want to stop children from saying no instead of using this opportunity to help children learn to take responsibility for what happens in their daily lives. Some children are too compliant and are more likely to be chosen as victims. This is especially true for children with disabilities, but we must be careful not to teach over compliance to all children. Even if a child is very dependent on the parent for many aspects of their care, it is important to give the child opportunities to say no in appropriate situations. You need to teach your child that she can say 'no' to the little things in her life so that one day she will be able to say 'no' to the big things in her life if she needs to. As Dave Hingsburger writes in his book Just Say Know, "People who can't say no to peas will never understand their right to say no to a penis".

Parents actually begin to teach children about yes and no from the day of the child's birth. Every time your child cries because she is wet and every time you pick up your crying child to comfort her, you are responding to the baby communicating discomfort with her current situation. In essence when a baby cries, she is saying "No. I don't like it." When a caretaker responds, we tell the child they have some control in their life. We are teaching trust and security as well.

As your child grows, start to look for opportunities which are acceptable to you to begin teaching your child to say 'no'. For example, you might give your toddler a choice of cereals to have for breakfast.

    DAD: "John, you may have Cheerios or Corn Puffs today."
    John: no response
    DAD: "Do you want Cheerios?"

John: "NO"
DAD: "You don't want Cheerios. That's fine.
Here are your Corn Puffs."

This is a simple example and you can probably find many opportunities to teach your child choice-making. You can also find many opportunities to respect your child's wishes when she says 'no'. When your child is able to understand more complex language, provide more than two choices when possible.

If your child cannot say yes or no, she may shake her head, use sign language or a gesture, make a face or a sound, push something away from her, etc. There are many ways to communicate. Be very careful that if you offer a choice that it really is a choice. If you give a choice and then take it away, this is very confusing for your child. It may teach her that saying 'No' is really not allowed.

> One day a four year old child was playing with his toys when his mom asked, "Would you like to go to the store with me?" The child said 'no'. A couple minutes later, the mother reached her hand out and said, "Let's go". The child had a temper tantrum. Obviously this boy understood about choices and saying 'no' and did not like his choice being taken away.

In addressing the needs of a child who cannot talk, skills can still be taught. For example, the child who pushes the dish across the table because she doesn't want the food that is on it, is communicating very clearly…without words. We can teach the skills of saying 'no' by offering choices and then helping the child to point, push, nod, sign, etc. This is easier to teach if you are 'listening' to your child as we discussed earlier. Your child might make a face or move her eyes in a certain way when she wants to communicate "no". If you notice this and let her know that you understand she is saying "no", she will be less likely to exhibit more extreme behaviors, like throwing things. Here's an example: Bob was sitting on the floor and playing with a toy. His sister came over and sat real close to him. He made a face. Then he grunted. Then he pushed her and she started crying. The face he made and the grunting sound may have been his way of saying "No, I don't want you so close to me". When we can respond before the pushing is necessary for Bob to communicate his feelings, we teach him that he can say "NO" in a manner which makes life much easier, for the parent, for Bob and for his sister.

There is research that indicates that children who are taught to be overly compliant are at greater risk of sexual abuse. In other words, people who are taught to always do whatever they are told to do, by anyone who tells them are more likely to be abused. We must be careful not to teach over compliance to all children. This means that we need to teach children when and how to say "NO". If your child can talk, teach her to say no loud and clear if she is in danger. You can practice this with her using different role plays. Praise her for being firm in her responses.

LANGUAGE FOR BODY PARTS

There comes a time in your child's development when you need to begin to teach the names of the parts of the body. Our private body parts are the parts of our body that a swimsuit covers. As you teach your child the names of her body parts, use the correct terms. We usually do this for the eyes, ears, hair, nose, hands, etc. but not for the private body parts. We make up all kinds of slang words for the penis, scrotum and vulva. You might be uncomfortable saying the words penis or vagina to your small child and that is okay. We believe that it is best to teach the names of the body parts which you are comfortable with during the same time you teach names for the private body parts. A good time to do this is during normal activities when the body is exposed, such as bath time. Teach your child the word by pointing to the body part and saying the proper term: "Here are your eyes"…"Here is your penis", etc. Try and use the same facial expression when naming each part. For example, don't make a face when you say penis as you don't want to teach your child that the penis is bad. It is okay to speak in a quieter tone of voice when teaching private body parts. This may actually help your child learn that these are private and not to be discussed in public.

I taught my daughter from the very beginning the proper terms for her body parts. We had company one night when she was barely 2 years of age. She was the only child present and was taking advantage of the attention by 'performing' her vast motor skills for us. In the middle of an elaborate, toddler dance routine she slipped and fell to the floor and immediately screamed, "I hurt my vagina!" I'll admit that our company was shocked to hear the word vagina from such a small child and my husband and I looked at each other with that 'this is so funny but we can't laugh' look. My daughter and I went to a private room to check for injuries.

Eventually your child may be able to point to the body part when you say the word (i.e., "Show me your eyes", etc.). When this happens, a big smile from you and a "good girl!" is important to reinforce the child's learning. Even if your child doesn't learn to say or sign the word or point to the body part, it is still important that you continue to associate the body part with the word for the body part. She may understand what you are saying even if she can't communicate it back to you.

When we talk with our children about their private body parts, we are giving them the power to tell if someone hurts them in a sexual manner. By teaching them about their genitals, we give them permission to discuss this part of their body and we also give them the tools to discuss this part of their body. There have been situations in which people had medical problems in their 'private areas' and treatment was delayed because they had no language to communicate the problem and/or because they had learned to be ashamed of that part of their bodies. We do not want that to happen to your child.

> There was a child who called his penis a 'doodey'. He was listening to an adult talk about all of the responsibilities in the adults' life and the adult said, "I have so many duties I can't do them all." The child looked up at his mom and said, "Why does she have so many doodies? I only need one to pee."

As your child grows older, you might choose to teach the body function which goes with the body parts. For example, "You see with your eyes…you pee from your urethra." Have you ever wondered why the words for the private body parts are more difficult to say? We have! Eyes and ears are so much easier to say than urethra or testicles. Oh well!

If your child is around someone who is expecting a baby, a wonderful opportunity exists for teaching. Please do not tell your child that babies grow in their Mommy's tummy! Babies grow in the uterus (or womb). We need to trust children with information. We need to provide accurate, honest information. When something important happens in your child's life, we want her to trust you with the information. This is more likely to happen if you have established a pattern of trusting them with information.

Orieda was teaching human sexuality to a grade school class when one young boy asked, "My mom has a baby in her tummy. How come the baby doesn't get all poopie when my mom goes to the bathroom?"

When your child is approaching puberty, you can teach then about pubic hair, breast development and menses for the girls and wet dreams for the boys. If your child is not told about normal body functions, he or she may get confused or scared when their bodies begin to change. It is best to tell them about these changes **before** they occur. **We know you may not want to do this!!!** We know that this is difficult and embarrassing for most parents. There are some books which might be of some help to you and we have listed some in the back for you to consider. It may be easier for you to read a book to your child than to find your own words to talk about this. You might also choose to read a book for yourself to make you more comfortable about the topic before you speak with your child. You can also see if the school has someone who can help. It is perfectly natural to be embarrassed about things which are so private. It is okay to tell your child that it is embarrassing. This helps your child understand that it can be difficult to talk about private things.

I was conducting a sexuality workshop and asked the audience what words they used as children for their genitals. I heard the usual responses. At the break a man approached me to tell me that when he was a child he referred to his genitals as 'self'. I had never heard that one before and asked him to explain. He said, "Well, my parents always told me 'Don't touch yourself! Don't play with yourself! Keep yourself clean!" I laughed and told him he would read about this in one of my books one day. Thanks for sharing!

HEALTHY AND UNHEALTHY TOUCH

Before we talk about how to teach your child the difference between healthy and unhealthy touch, we want to discuss the importance of touch in your child's life. Your baby needs your touch to develop muscles, to grow, to learn and to feel loved and safe. Hold your baby several times a day. Talk to your baby while holding her, feeding her, and changing her diaper. When you touch your baby, it is good for both your baby and for you. You are preparing your baby for her future. When you touch your child you are beginning to teach your child about feelings, love and affection. Each child's need for touch may be different. Do your best to understand your child's need for touch and affection. Be sure to give your child attention even when she is not demanding it. Talk to her and/ or touch her even when she is playing quietly. Touch is important to your child's growth and feeling of security. Healthy touches from you include holding an infant or toddler, hugs, hand holding, touch on shoulder, foot rubs, etc. It is important for parents to do this!! This is how we teach children about healthy touch.

Unhealthy touch is any touch which makes the child uncomfortable. Bad touch is not limited to touching of private body parts. This is a mistake we have made in the past. Some people have been taught that it is okay to touch or be touched anywhere but 'private parts' and that is not true. There are other places on your body that someone can touch and make you uncomfortable...you get to choose who touches you, how and where you are touched...and so should your child. Instead of teaching good and bad touch (or safe and unsafe touch) according to body parts, let's teach it according to how it makes us feel. We will talk about the exceptions later but here are some guidelines:
- Good touch makes you feel happy and warm inside.
- Bad touch can hurt and it might make you cry or feel mad.

If your child feels uncomfortable with a touch, she has the right to say "Stop!" or "NO!" or to push someone away or to make a loud noise. Practice this with your toddler. Children learn best if we teach in a variety of ways. For example:

- We talk about saying no to some touches.
- We show how to say no.
- We practice saying no.
- We respect the child's no in real situations.

Some parents make a game out of this by using dolls. Your child may learn by watching this kind of demonstration. Children are good at imitating what they see you do. We are sure that you can come up with creative ways to teach these skills in a manner that works best for you and your child.

Let your child know that if someone makes her feel bad, she can tell you. You can teach your child that she can tell you anything and not get in trouble. An important message is "You will not get in trouble for what someone else does". Let your child know that you want her to be safe and that you will help her if she has a problem.

It is often reported by a victim of childhood sexual abuse that an early attempt was made to tell a parent about their abuse but the child did not feel listened to so the disclosure was not made. Because it is so very difficult to tell a parent that someone is sexually abusing them, the child's initial attempt may be subtle. Your response to this first attempt, will determine if your child continues to tell you what is on their mind. The child might say, "Uncle Joe is bad." And if the parent responds with "No he isn't! You know Uncle Joe gave you that great toy", the child may not say anymore. It would be better to say something like, "You think Uncle Joe is bad? What has he done that makes you say that?" The attempts at disclosure may include comments such as "Something bad is happening in my bedroom" or "I don't want to go to Bill's.

He's nasty." Or "Grandpa keeps me awake at night" or "My stomach hurts."

Some children talk so much that parents sometimes give acknowledging responses, like "uh, huh" without even really hearing what the child says. You might consider having a code between you and your child that means THIS IS REALLY SERIOUS. You can make up a word that signals you to stop and sit with your child and listen. You might use the same 'emergency' word that you all agreed to use if you ever have to send someone else to tell your child something or pick them up from day care. So if your emergency word is KUDOS, and you are doing dishes and your child comes up, tugs on your pants and says "kudos", you know it's time to pay close attention.

Confusing feelings can happen about whether touch is good or bad. A child who has not received enough nurturing or touching, may allow bad touches - just to have touching in her life. We have worked with people who have such an intense need for touching that they will allow or even seek out touch which is harmful, just to have some touching! Try and make sure that your child has enough 'good touching' in her life so that this is less likely to happen to her. A child may also be confused when she really likes spending time with a person but does not like it when the person abuses her. The child may enjoy playing games and eating ice cream with an abuser but not like the way he touches her. This may result in feeling all mixed up and also makes it harder for the child to 'tell' on the abuser.

Touching for personal care and medical procedures is necessary for your child's general health. It helps your child to understand these kinds of touch when they occur in specific settings/routines. Limit the number of people who provide personal care procedures which involve the private parts of the child's body. When your child gets older, be sure that personal care is provided in private areas. For example, bathing, dressing, diaper changing of a child who is three or older should be done in rooms with doors closed or at least with visual barriers to protect the child's privacy. To the extent possible, try to use the same medical professionals for your child's health care needs. Some people assure that these procedures occur only when the care provider is wearing a lab coat so the child learns to associate the 'okay' procedure with the lab coat. (This is not a fail proof technique.) You can also request that gloves be worn when any touching of private body parts is necessary to keep a barrier between your child's skin and the care provider's skin. These last procedures are most important for children with disabilities who may have extensive medical and personal care procedures performed for an extended period of time. In this situation, we must take extra care to teach privacy of and respect for the child's body.

It is natural for a child to explore her own body. If your son touches his penis while you are changing his diaper or your daughter touches her vulva while you are changing her diaper, remember that **this is normal.** Your response when this happens is very important. If you make a disapproving face and yell "Stop that!", you will teach your child that this area of their body is bad. Instead, you might say, "When you are fresh and clean, you may touch your penis (or vulva) because we are in a private place." Every part of your child is precious. Be careful with your language, facial expression and tone of voice while changing diapers and when your child touches herself. This is the beginning of teaching about healthy body image and privacy.

I was at the theatre one night and noticed a young mother holding a baby in one arm and trying to help her toddler put on a coat with her 'free' hand. I asked if she needed any help and the toddler said, "No. You are a stranger!" I told the mother, "What wonderful training you have done and I thank you!"

CHOICES REGARDING TYPES OF TOUCH

Think about some of the people in your life and the many ways in which they communicate their feelings to you. Can somebody show you they care about you without touching you? Of course they can. Some people seem to not understand this and it gets them in trouble. Some people want to hug everyone they come into contact with and we need to teach children that there are many choices when it comes to greeting skills as well as ways to express affection. The most common ways to express affection are: eye contact, smile, wave, "high five", sign language, touch on the shoulder, handshake, spending time together and hugs. You might want to teach your toddler that hugs are for the really special people in her life. This becomes more important as your child gets older. Teach your child that she can choose how to communicate with others and there are many okay choices.

The Director of an Early Intervention program in Illinois was making a home visit one afternoon with one of her staff. The visit was to a new family to the agency and when the parent opened the door, introductions were made and everyone shook hands. Once inside the home, the parent introduced the two-year-old who put his hand out for a hand shake also. Clearly, this child understood the different touch options available to him. Kudos to these parents!

One of the most important things you can teach your child is that she has the right to choose who touches her. **Never force your child to hug or kiss someone!** Respect your child's choice about who she wants to touch, whom she allows to touch her and when she wants to be touched. It might hurt grandma's feelings if your child does not want to hug her and it might embarrass you but you need to respect your child's choice on this. If your child has learned some of the above touch options, you can suggest one of them to ease the situation. For example, "Give grandma one of your big smiles" or "Give grandma a 'high five'!" Your child could have lots of reasons for not wanting to hug someone. The person might have bad breath. The person might hold too tight. The child might not be in the mood for a hug right now. We may never know the reason and that's okay. The important thing is to trust your child to trust her own feelings about who touches her body and then honor her choices.

> *When my daughter was about three years old, she taught me a lesson as only a child can. We were visiting her aunt and as most adults do, I said "Go give Aunt Judy a hug and kiss". Well, my daughter went up to her aunt and looked more or less like a rag doll. She did not hug her, but she was swallowed up by her aunt's big breasts. At this point she stated, "Mommy I don't like this". We talked about it later and she was able to explain what made her feel uncomfortable and what she did not like about the hug. We came up with a substitution for the hug and from that point on, I have let my children express themselves in ways that they choose.*

If your child cannot directly express her choices regarding touch, pay attention to her signs that she may not want to be touched by someone. Does your child make a face of discomfort? Does she turn a shoulder away? If she indicates displeasure in any way, you can suggest a different choice such as a handshake, wave, high five, etc. With your help, your child can learn she has a choice.

> *He was a close friend of my grandson and had spent many hours at my house over the years. When he became an adult, he moved away, but always stopped by our home when he was in town. He stopped by with his wife and toddler one day and we had a delightful visit. I was referred to as grandma*

Anderson throughout the visit. As they were preparing to leave, he told his son, "Here, kiss grandma Anderson goodbye." The child hesitated and I said, "No. He doesn't know me." To which the father said to his son, "Oh, go ahead and kiss her." I firmly said, "NO. He doesn't need to kiss me. He already has my approval" and I turned to the child and said with a smile, "It was really nice to meet you."

If someone (an adult or older child) continues to hug (or tickle) your child despite your child's resistance, ask the other person to respect your child's wishes. This not only teaches your child how to stand up for herself but also teaches her that you will stand up for her as well. If it makes it easier, come up with some standard lines that you can use in these situations. Some examples might be:

- ❖ In our home, no means no, when it comes to touching.
- ❖ Please help us teach Sue that we respect her body.
- ❖ It is important to me that we respect John's right to choose who touches him.
- ❖ She doesn't want a hug right now.
- ❖ We don't touch without permission.
- ❖ We're teaching Pat that we respect her body. I could sure use your help.

If someone touches your child and your child turns away, it might be a good time to have your child practice saying no to touch she doesn't want. You might say to your child, "Cammie doesn't want to hug grandma right now?" When your child indicates no, then say, "Tell grandma 'not now please'". Praise your child if she follows through and make sure grandma respects the request.

SOCIAL DISTANCE

Children learn the rules of social distance as they develop. Most people like a comfortable distance between them and others during social interaction. Although this can vary from person to person and within cultures, the average distance is about an arm's length. Some people are not taught this unwritten rule and may stand very close to others. This can cause problems when your child is an adolescent or an adult. These rules of social distance can begin to be learned in early childhood.

We begin teaching social distance through our own behavior. We do not have to be in a child's face to talk with her or to get her attention. Be sure and teach your child that she can get your attention without grabbing you or always being close. When you feel that your child is old enough, you can make a game out of this. Games such as London Bridge, Hide and Seek, Tag and Ring Around the Rosie can all teach some of the rules about social distance. These games can be adapted for children with disabilities so they can be included. It is also important to make note of social distance in everyday activities. For example: "this is how close I stand when we dance...when we talk...when we wait in line at the store", etc. You can teach your child about the 'arm's length rule' just by practicing with her. A child who requires extended assistance with personal assistance still has the right to have social distance between her and other people.

As your child gets older, teach her not to touch younger children or strangers. In general, teach her to wave to children. Of course, there may be exceptions for siblings and others. Continue to teach her the arm's length rule and be a good role model.

She had always been a friendly child and her friendliness was frequently rewarded with smiles, kind words and big hugs. Her friendliness included lots of touching. As a teenager, she would smile and touch everyone she met…on the arm, shoulder, knee, etc. Unfortunately, her friendliness was taken advantage of by an older man who saw her as an easy target. Fortunately, she had observant parents and well-trained staff who intervened early in the situation. The abuse stopped before it had progressed to the point of rape and the man no longer has access to her.

RELATIONSHIPS

This factor in prevention of sexual abuse involves teaching the child that different people have different meaning in our life. Our parents take care of us. We have to share things with our brothers and sisters; like our toys and our parent's attention. Some people are nice to us and others are not so nice. We can trust some people but not others.

In the world of Special Education, the CIRCLES program is frequently used to teach students about different relationships and the corresponding rules of behavior. We have seen many children who have siblings with a disability embrace the CIRCLES program. The CIRCLES program uses color to symbolize each type of relationship; purple means private; blue means close hug; green means far away hug; yellow means handshake, orange means wave and red means stop (stranger circle). If you choose to use the CIRCLES program, you can teach your child these ideas by the specific people in his/her life. For example, Mom is in the close hug circle (blue) and the fireman wears a uniform and a badge and is in the stranger circle (red). A picture can be made out of construction paper and hung in the child's bedroom to help teach and remind the child of the essential lessons.

A community agency in Illinois worked hard to teach teens and adults with disabilities about relationships. The CIRCLES program was used on a regular basis to teach these concepts. A counselor began to make 'CIRCLE boards' as a teaching tool. A CIRCLE board is a round board with the colored circles; each has a different texture so the board can be used with persons who are visually impaired. The counselor would have one of the persons she was working with help glue the colored textures on the board and teach the different relationships at the same time. After completing one of the CIRCLE boards, the counselor and the individual who helped, presented the board to one of the 'bosses' in the agency. This was an opportunity for the individual to be thanked for her help and to practice what she had learned. She described each circle, beginning with, "Purple is me, blue is my family, etc." When the 'boss' praised her, she leaned over to kiss the boss who then asked, "What circle are we in?" The young woman backed up, smiled and put her hand out for a shake. These concepts take longer to teach when individuals have been hugging everyone for many years. This young woman needs more training and the family and agency will keep working with her.

While the CIRCLES program is simple and concrete, giving parameters, you can certainly teach your child about relationships during the normal course of life. You do this by modeling and active teaching. By modeling the differences in your own relationships, your child will see that you do not treat everyone the same way. Your child will notice that you treat her differently that you do other people's children; that you treat your best friend differently than you treat a teacher, the minister or grocery clerk. Through active teaching, you tell your child the rules you want her to use with different people in her life. You teach about brothers, sisters, grandparents, neighbors, acquaintances, and strangers. This is related to teaching about social distance, touch options, healthy and unhealthy touch and privacy. It all fits together...trust, touch, and talk.

You can also begin to teach your child about secrets when she is a toddler. This is what you can tell your child:

Good secrets feel good inside. A good secret is often about a surprise for someone; like a birthday present for grandpa. Bad secrets feel 'yucky' or confusing inside. A secret that feels bad or confusing should be told. If someone offers you a gift to keep a secret, it is probably a bad secret.

Teach the concept of secrets through everyday examples and storytelling. There is a book called <u>The Trouble with Secrets</u> by Karen Johnson, which can be read with your child. (See more information in the resource list on this book.)

It is important that you teach your child to trust her feelings about people and about secrets. If it makes her feel bad, it is not a secret that should be kept. A safe person should be told. A safe person is an adult who can help her.

TEACHING PRIVACY

What does privacy include? When we think about teaching children about privacy, there are categories to consider: private body parts, private locations, private activities/ behavior and private conversations. We can start to teach about privacy at an early age. The first thing to do is to evaluate your own habits within your home. Ask yourself the following questions:

- Do you close the bedroom door when changing clothes?
- Do you close the bathroom door when taking a bath or shower? When using the toilet?
- Do you discuss private topics in front of the children?
- Do you 'make out' with your spouse or partner in front of the children?
- Do you speak about private things in public places, such as the store?

Your behavior teaches your child what is acceptable and what is not. Your home is your castle, so the saying goes, but once you have a child, you need to evaluate what you should and should not do in front of your children. This is how you teach your children about boundaries.

The next step is to actively teach your child about the concept of privacy. When your child is a toddler, begin introducing the word "private" into your daily activities. When taking your child to the bathroom for a bath or for toilet training, close the door and say, "This is private so the door is closed". As your child grows, involve your child in assuring privacy. For example, when the time is right, and if your child is able to, you can say something like "Your bath is private. Would you close the door please?" Later you might say, "It's bath time. What should we do so we are private?" The main way to teach about privacy is by matching the word private with the activity and by being a good role model!! If you leave the door open when you use the bathroom but teach your child to close the door when she uses the bathroom, the child will be confused abut what to do. Most often the child will learn to do what she sees you do, not what you say to do.

As your child approaches the age of three or four, you will want to take further steps to teach your child about privacy and modesty. Children learn modesty at different ages and even If your child docs not exhibit the need for modesty, we feel it is important for you to actively teach modesty to your child by the age of four. Around this time, you can start teaching your child that her private body parts are to be covered in front of company, siblings, etc. It is equally important around this age, that the child not see their parents or other adults in the nude.

If you have a child with a disability, it is critically important that you take extra steps to teach her about privacy. If your child's disability means that you have to help with wiping, washing their penis or vulva, diaper changing, etc., you will still need to teach about privacy. By the age of four, be sure that these activities are performed where others cannot see. We often change babies' diapers in the living room. Some children with disabilities need to wear diapers indefinitely and we need to remember that we cannot teach privacy if we change their diapers on the living room floor in front of company. Be sensitive to your child's feelings about having to wear diapers or have assistance and do not make statements about this in front of anyone that might embarrass your child. Make sure that doors are closed and that your child is clearly taught the rules of privacy. Even if you think it doesn't matter to your child, this is a teaching moment of great importance!!

We can usually teach about private locations along with teaching about private body parts and private activities/ behavior. Private behavior includes: going to the bathroom, bathing, showering, and touching private body parts. These behaviors are done in private locations. Any behavior which exposes our private body parts must be done in private locations. Just what is a private location? We typically think of bedrooms and bathrooms as private but are ALL bedrooms private? What if the bedroom is shared with others? Is there a difference between what we can do in our bathroom at home and what we can do in the bathroom at the mall or theatre? As your child gets older, it may be important for you to teach your child these distinctions. A bedroom is private if no one can see you. If a child or adult is in a bedroom alone with the door closed, but standing in front of a window with the curtains open, it is not private. If your child spends the night with friends or cousins, and several people are sharing a bedroom, it is not private. In this case, the child may want to change clothes in the bathroom, with the doors closed of course. If your child learns these distinctions at some point, her risk for sexual abuse decreases. What if your child has a disability? We know that not every child with a disability can learn all of these skills, but if your child has learned the basics about private and public, try to teach the skills in this paragraph as well.

In teaching about private locations, it is helpful to let your child know which people can be with them in a private location. As the parent, spend some time thinking about who you would want to give permission to bathe your child or help with toilet training, etc. You have the responsibility for establishing the boundaries for your child when they are little. Once you have made these decisions, you can share this information with your child as you teach them about privacy. Review the names with your child from time to time and let them have input into the persons who can help them with such private matters. This process communicates respect and dignity for your child and their body.

One of the things we tend not to consider in teaching private versus public is that of conversations. You probably know the 'rules' about what is okay to discuss in front of others and which topics are more private in nature. We need to make a concerted effort to teach our children what things should only be discussed in private. This can get tricky as once a child enters day care or the world of special education, just about everything is discussed in front of the children. As a parent, you may have to work really hard to make sure the concept of private information does not get lost. You have a right to privacy of information and so does your child. If your child is verbal, it is important that she learn what not to discuss in the school hallways or at church or in the waiting room at the doctor's office or the grocery store checkout.

Again, the first step is to be a good role model for your child. Try not to have personal, private conversations in front of your children. If you are having an intimate discussion with your mate, think about who is around that might hear. The next step is to actively teach your verbal child about private talk. Teaching the concept of private talk includes WHAT is being discussed, WHERE it is being discussed, and with WHOM it is being discussed. This may sound complicated, but can actually begin when your child is a toddler. Gently encourage your children to discuss their bowel movements and their 'butts' in private locations. If your child learns this skill when she is young, it will probably carry over to adolescence and adulthood.

Many adolescents and adults with disabilities will discuss their dates, abuse, private body parts, family business and everything else around anyone. This increases their vulnerability to people who might be looking for someone to abuse. It also makes other people uncomfortable and they may not want to be around your child. We have found it is fairly simple to change this habit by using a consistent message of "That is private. We need to be in a private room to discuss it." Then we add the concept of safe person. "We only discuss private things with safe people." A safe person is a grown up who will not hurt your child but will help your child when she has a problem and someone who believes what your child says. You can help your child make a list of her 'safe people', so you both know who they are. Once a child knows about private talk and safe people, you can check with her from time to time. If Uncle John has been added to her safe person list, you can check and see what that means.

Julie was a young person who had been sexually abused. She saw me in the hallway one day and began to tell me about the abuse. I quietly told her, "This is private. Let's go to a private place." When we got to my office, I closed the door and said, "The door is closed so no one can hear. This is a private place. You can tell me now." A few days later I saw Julie in the hall again. She started to talk and then put her hand on her mouth. She removed her hand and whispered, "Oh, it's private. Can we go to your office?" I was amazed at how quickly she had learned the lesson

SECTION 3

BOYS AND GIRLS

When there is great love, there are miracles.

Unknown

Boys and Girls

When a person or a couple discover that they are going to have a baby, one of the first things they wonder about is the sex of the child. Will this baby be a boy or a girl? When prospective parents tell others about the impending birth, what is the first question they are asked? Exactly! "Do you want a boy or a girl? Some people have a strong preference about the gender and express disappointment if the baby is not the gender they wanted. It might be helpful for you to review your own opinions about the gender of your baby.

- Was the gender important to you?
- If so, why was it so important?
- Is your baby the gender you wanted?
- What is different if you have a child with a gender other than the one you wanted?
- Why is the gender so important to so many of us?

But perhaps the most important question for us to think about is:
- What are my expectations for a boy child?
- What are my expectations for a girl child?

Our expectations are directly related to how we rear our children. There is plenty of evidence that people respond very differently to little girls than to little boys. Some of these differences are directly related to the high frequency in which girls and women are the victims of sexual abuse (estimated 91%) and the high frequency in which boys and men are the offenders of sexual abuse (nearly 99%). Given these statistics, it is logical to say that boys and men play a critical role in the prevention of sexual assaults.

Given what we know about sexual violence, we feel that we can help reduce these numbers by raising children who are empowered and assertive and value equality among the sexes. We are not saying that boys and girls are the same...we are saying that all children have equal value. Think about that. We might be able to raise children who can reduce the incidence of sexual violence in our world! What an awesome thought!!

Since my daughter was an infant, people have always stopped to tell her how beautiful she is. I could always tell that it bothered her; even before she could talk I noticed how her expression would turn to annoyance and sometimes anger. This always embarrassed me as her mother. I wanted her to smile and respond 'appropriately'.

When she became old enough to talk and express herself, we continued to teach her to be polite and say thank you when strangers approached and told her how pretty she was. She rarely did so and again would look annoyed. At times she even responded, "I don't care".

I suppose it is important to stress how often the comments occur...ALL OF THE TIME. Anytime we go to a restaurant, the store, the mall, etc., several people will stop to comment on her beautiful appearance. I never really understood why she was so rude to people or why she did not respond happily. Is it really so bad to have people tell you that you are beautiful all of the time? We should all have such big problems.

Since she has grown and just started school, I have noticed something. When a person tells her that she is smart, or a good soccer player, or that she is a good, nice girl...she beams and responds politely with "Thank you". She loves helping people and doing things for others, and is so happy when she sees that she has made a difference.

*I realize that she wants to be a good person who is doing "important" things, not simply a person who is 'pretty' on the outside. This never made her happy. What makes her happy is when we stress the good **in** her, not on the outside of her.*

What are some ways that girls and boys are reared that perpetuate girls being victims?

Girls
- ◆ Focus on physical appearance
- ◆ Focus on being sensitive to others feelings
- ◆ Focus on expressing feelings
- ◆ Focus on understanding others
- ◆ Focus on compromise
- ◆ Focus on family
- ◆ Focus on nurturing others

Boys
- ◆ Focus on physical abilities
- ◆ Focus on being tough
- ◆ Focus on keeping feelings inside
- ◆ Focus on solving problems
- ◆ Focus on competition
- ◆ Focus on money
- ◆ Focus on protecting others

We recognize that there have been many changes in the traditional roles of men and women but we do continue to see major differences in how parents and society respond to boys and girls. As we began writing this section, these are the questions we faced:

- How can we bring up children who will grow up and view each other as equals? (no matter what the gender, race, disability, sexual orientation, economic status, etc.)

- How can we rear little boys who can express their feeling and will take action to stop violence against girls and women?
- How can we bring up little girls who can honor their feelings and are empowered to be who they are?

We teach first by what we model. Our children learn to imitate us at an early age. They learn about our values and our prejudices. Your children can tell by your behavior how you feel about family, money, sex roles, religion, violence, different races, discipline, etc. So first, we need to look at ourselves. Your children listen when you speak to someone on the phone. They notice your comments about characters on television. They *really* pay attention to how you treat them in relation to their siblings. Their ears perk up when they think you might be talking about them and they certainly know how you act when you are mad. In other words, "they don't miss much".

Here are some general guidelines which we believe are beneficial for your children:

- Perhaps the most important protective factor to raising a child who is not violent is the bonding that occurs between parent and child during early development. A strong, consistent emotional attachment is critical for a child to feel safe and secure. Infants need lots of attention; they need to know that their needs and cries are responded to. This is how they develop trust. You cannot spoil a baby.
- Evaluate your own ability to express feelings in an appropriate manner. Role model expressing feelings including fear and disappointment as well as joy and love. Encourage your child (boy and /or

girl) to express their emotions. Some people need to "walk it out" before they can "talk it out".

- Select books, electronic games and television shows that are appropriate to the child's age. Participate WITH your child and discuss the characters, topics and situations; discuss the TV shows and how the show relates to your child. Actively teach what is most important in your family.
- If your child sees or hears something violent or inappropriate in your presence, discuss your feelings about the situation with her.
- Listen to music with your child. As your child gets older, if he listens to music which is violent, share your thoughts with him.
- Encourage the solving of problems which emphasizes mutual listening and compromise. When there is a disagreement, ask each person to state how they think the other person feels. Praise your child when they understand the other persons' point of view. This teaches empathy, listening and peaceful problem-resolution.
- Encourage your child to develop skills based on their unique interests and talents; not based on their gender. Communicate to your children how special they are. For boys, emphasize nonviolent ways to express their feelings or girls, emphasize expressing their selves and their needs.
- Be sure and tell your child that "hands are not for hitting"; especially boys who get conflicting messages about what it means to be a man. There is an organization called *Men Can Stop Rape* and their media campaign includes the slogan, "My strength is not for hurting". Perhaps we should teach our boys "Your strength Is for helping".
- Model nonviolence and equality in your own relationships. Your child is watching.

We have these precious lives in our hands. We have the power to influence new lives. We have incredible responsibility. As we start and continue this journey, let's refocus our attention. See the difference in the list from the previous list on page 75:

BOYS AND GIRLS

- Focus on expressing feelings whether happy, sad, scared or mad.
- Focus on understanding others as well as standing up for oneself.
- Focus on the family.
- Focus on working as a team to solve problems which help everyone.
- Focus on treating everyone with equality… everyone. Teach to be fair and share.
- Focus on everyone's uniqueness as a person.
- Focus on each person's power and contribution to the family.
- Focus on developing emotional attachments which nurture a safe environment.

Why all of the focus on equality? Because sexual abuse is about power, not about sex. It is an act in which someone uses power to control another person. If we teach our children to have personal power because of their own uniqueness, they won't feel powerless or learn to TAKE power from others. If we teach our children that all humans deserve to have equal power, we take positive action to reduce violence in our society. So teach your children to be fair and share and show respect for self and others.

If your child has a disability, you might be wondering how this section applies to you and your child. This section applies to ALL children. If you have a baby girl with cerebral palsy, she is a baby girl first…and above all else. Girls and women with disabilities still consider their femaleness as a core element of who they are. Boys and men with disabilities still consider their maleness as a core element of who they are. Perhaps the most important message of this chapter is that all people are of equal value…ALL children have value. Boys and girls - equal value. Children with disabilities and children without disabilities - equal value. Children with poor families and children with rich families - equal value. And so it goes…our children are precious and valuable.

Again, we are not saying that boys and girls are the same. We believe that part of a child's identity is his/her gender. Being female is a part of who I am. I like being a woman and I don't know what it feels like to be a man. In the same way, being male is part of a man's identity. Boys and girls have equal value and contribute equally to the world. Establishing a world in which all people have equal value is a key in reducing violence. You play an important role in making this happen.

CREATING SAFE ENVIRONMENTS IN GROUP SETTINGS - SKILLS

One generation plants trees; Another gets the shade.
                                        Chinese Proverb

This section of the book is designed specifically for people who provide care to preschool children in group settings. This includes preschools and day care providers; three to five special education programs; church nurseries; licensed baby-sitters; YWCA and YMCA programs; respite centers; early intervention services; residential services; Head Start programs and others.

Parents are encouraged to work closely with these providers to establish safe environments for their children.

One day I picked up my 5-year old daughter from preschool. We went through our usual "How was your day?" conversation. However, this day, it took quite a different turn when she told me, "Tommy kissed my privacy today." At first her words didn't really sink in so I asked her to repeat the statement. Again, she said to me that one of her classmates had kissed her in her "privacy".

Here I am driving my van, trying not to over react or frighten my child, but I was very concerned. I have worked for the last eight years for an organization which serves children and adults with disabilities. I know that people take advantage of the people we serve and I am sensitive to these issues.

When we got home, I asked my daughter to show me where the little boy had "kissed" her. She pointed to her upper thigh, very near her vagina, or as she referred to 'her privacy'. I also asked her to explain where and when the incident occurred, as well as what her teachers were doing at the time. My daughter was sitting next to several boys during story time and it happened while her teacher was reading to the class. When I asked why she didn't tell her teacher, her response was that she didn't want to interrupt her teacher.

I gently told my daughter that this was serious and that she can interrupt someone to ask for help when someone touches her private areas. I spoke to my husband when he got home and he, too, was concerned. We decided to contact the teacher and possibly the director of the preschool in the morning.

I explained to the teacher what my daughter had told me the previous evening. I expressed my appreciation that the nurse had taught the children about ok and not ok touch. I also expressed my concerns about this young boy's behavior. The teacher told me that this little boy acts up a lot, which I knew from conversations with my daughter. The teacher also said that since my daughter did not tell her immediately, that this boy could not be disciplined for his behavior.

I again told my daughter that if anything like this ever happens again that she must tell an adult IMMEDIATELY, even if it means interrupting a story or lesson at school.

As a parent, the whole situation made me feel very helpless. I appreciated my child's candor in telling me what happened, but talking to the teacher didn't offer me closure or reassurance that something like this wouldn't happen to my child again.

In the situation above, the parent had read our <u>Genesis: In the Beginning...Breaking the Cycle of Sexual Abuse</u> and contacted us for direction. The following suggestions were made:

1. Contact the Director of the preschool and discuss your concerns. Give them a copy of the Genesis book and ask that the Director share the information with all of the staff and incorporate the skills training into the preschool environment. The Director should also contact the local Sexual Assault Center and request prevention education classes for the children.

2. Encourage the preschool to purchase copies of It's My Body by Lory Freeman and incorporate it into the reading program at the preschool.
3. Follow up with the teacher to see what has happened.

The story is a common one and parents often feel helpless when something like this occurs. In reality, most preschool teachers have not had training related to sexual abuse prevention. Most preschool teachers really like children and are doing the best they can given their knowledge, experience and guidance. This section is designed to assist preschool teachers, day care providers, baby-sitters, supervisors' of play groups, prevention initiatives, and early intervention programs, as well as church nurseries, preschool special education programs and others in developing safe environments for our young children.

It is a privilege to provide supervision and care to a young child. If you are responsible for the care of preschool children, we are grateful to you and want you to recognize the incredible role you play in each of their lives. Your mood and your interactions set the tone for the entire group. Make it a personal goal to have a positive interaction with each and every child on a daily basis. Each child needs some personal attention and in some settings, the children who are the most active and verbal, get all of the attention. Make a special effort to engage the shy and quiet children and the children who don't demand your attention. Try to understand and acknowledge each child's unique qualities. The following quote eloquently describes your responsibility and power.

> "I've come to a frightening conclusion that I am the decisive element in the classroom. It's my personal approach that creates the climate. It's my daily mood that makes the weather. As a teacher, I possess a tremendous power to

make a child's life miserable or joyous. I can humiliate or humor, hurt or heal. In all situations, it is my response that decides whether a crisis will be escalated or de-escalated and a child humanized or dehumanized." Haim Ginott in Between Teacher and Child.

WOW! That's a lot of responsibility, huh? Remember that the setting in which you work is an extension of the child's home. You are responsible for providing a safe and nurturing environment. Review the section on listening as an important element of teaching.

Teaching the prevention skills to preschool children in group settings can become a natural part of your role as a teacher with a little practice. The skills that you want to teach and reinforce include: expression of feelings, privacy, saying 'no', language for body parts, touches, social distance, and different relationships. These are the same skills that we want parents to teach their children in the home. If the same skills are taught across different environments, the child is more likely to learn them well and understand their value.

TEACHING SMALL CHILDREN ABOUT FEELINGS IN A GROUP SETTING

You can utilize visual aids in the setting to assist you in this task. There are many 'feelings posters' on the market and having one posted in the environment is a useful tool. You can also use a group activity to make a poster of the four basic feelings. Have children look for pictures in magazines which show people who are MAD, SAD, HAPPY and SCARED. Put all of the happy pictures in one area of the poster; the sad pictures in another area, etc. Post the picture on the wall.

Each morning, when all the children arrive, you can go to the poster and ask each child how they are feeling. Include yourself in this activity and remember that you are a role model for the children. You can have each child point to the poster which represents how they feel and say their feelings. For example, the child points to the sad section of the poster and says, "I feel sad." You can ask the other children, "How does Susie feel?" This reinforces listening and empathy. You can also talk about what things we can do when we are sad to feel better. This 'check in' activity not only teaches children about expressing their feelings, but gives you valuable information about which children might need a little extra attention on a particular day.

You can also have children draw 'feeling faces'. You can use regular paper for this or you can have friends and family save the cardboard from frozen pizzas for you. These make great 'feeling faces'. You can keep them for use during the 'check in' activity or for use throughout the day. Each child can select the face which shows how they are feeling.

When reading books to children, you can stress the feelings of the various characters in the books. For example, if you are reading a story about a rabbit who has a big problem you

88   Safe Beginnings

can stop reading for a second and ask, "How does the rabbit feel?" Or you can say, "The rabbit is sad… Can you tell when someone is sad?…yes…Show me your sad faces… good…now let's see what the rabbit does."

These simple activities lay the foundation for identification and expression of feelings throughout the daily routine. When you see a child with a great big smile, you might say, "John, you look really happy!". When you see a child share a game with another child, you might say, "Maria, I am so happy that you are sharing with Billy." You will notice many opportunities to teach and reinforce the expression of feelings in your daily work with young children.

Many times when we see children 'acting out' with aggression, it is because of an uncomfortable feeling that the child is experiencing. If we can teach the child to identify the feeling (i.e., this is anger I am feeling) and express the feeling (i.e., "I am mad!"), the child can learn coping skills (e.g., "When I am mad, I can calm down if I sit by myself awhile"). Of course, each child will have a different set of coping skills that work for them but common ones include: talking about the feeling, being alone awhile, physical activity, and music. Teaching young children to identify and express their feelings is a first step in empowering them to be safe and assertive and to learn coping skills.

TEACHING PRIVACY

Privacy refers to:

- Private body parts (those that are covered by swim wear);
- Private locations (most rest rooms and bedrooms);
- Private activities (going to the rest room, baths, etc.); and
- Private talk (talk that is confidential or about private activities).

The best way to teach about privacy is during the normal course of the day. Private body parts should only be exposed in private locations. Private activities should only be done in private locations. If a child starts to pull their pants down before they reach the bathroom, quietly say, "That's private." and assist with covering them, if needed. If a child forgets to close the bathroom door when they are using the toilet, remind them to close the door. Use teachable moments to teach the concept of private and praise children when you see progress in their ability to secure privacy for themselves. Check your own behavior when it comes to assisting children who need your help with toileting, diaper changes, or changing clothes. If rules require a second staff member to be able to visually see the staff who is assisting with personal care, provide a screen so the concept of privacy can still be taught.

If you are providing care for a child who requires personal assistance such as diaper changing, beyond the typical age, be sure and provide privacy for those activities. Do not use "Well, he doesn't mind" as an excuse not to provide privacy. He *should* care and you can help teach him to care. We *want* him to care about his privacy. When you teach privacy, you teach respect for one's body. What an important lesson to learn.

Conversations about private topics should be held in areas in which the children can not hear. Staff should not be discussing their dates, marriages or sex lives with each other in front of children. If you are saying, "I'd never do that. What a stupid thing to say." Well, good for you. However, we have had experience with children who have become infatuated with sexual activity at an early age by listening to caretakers discuss their personal lives.

It is also important to remember not to discuss confidential information in front of the children. For example, you may be concerned about a mother who has mentioned her domestic abuse to you. This should not be discussed in front of any of the children.

If a child brings up a sexuality topic which seems beyond the age level of the child, please refer this situation to your director who will determine proper action to be taken.

TEACHING CHILDREN TO MAKE CHOICES AND SAY "NO"

Please review the prior section on "Saying NO". In a group setting, you are in a position to teach children boundaries. A boundary is a rule that cannot be broken without some consequence. A common rule is that children are not allowed to go into the street. A caretaker will do whatever is necessary to protect the child from the possible danger of being hit by a car. If we draw a circle around a child to represent the boundaries, outside the circle are the rules which cannot be broken. Inside the circle, there is flexibility. Inside the circle are the opportunities that you have to teach children how to say 'no'. (See illustration)

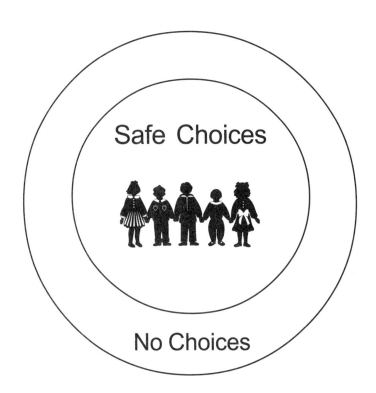

You can probably think of many examples within your setting to provide children with opportunities to say no and to make choices. Here are just a few examples of 'safe choices':

- Do you want ketchup for your fries?
- May I help you with your coat?
- Do you want me to read Mother Goose?
- Do you want crayons for your picture?
- Would you like to go outside and play? (when there is an option to go out or stay in).
- May I have a 'high five'?

When you ask a child a yes or no question, please honor their answer. This shows the child that they have some power in their life.

It is also possible to develop a group activity that teaches and reinforces the skill of saying 'no'. You can do mini skits of different situations n which children can practice saying 'no'. Here are some examples to get you started:

- A stranger approaches you at the park and asks if you want a piece of candy.
- Your uncle wants to give you a hug and you don't want to.
- A neighbor girl asks you to help her steal money from her mom's purse.
- A stranger asks you to come and help them look for their puppy.
- Your big brother wants you to clean his room for him.

Having children role play can be a lot of fun! When two children aro 'acting', have the others watch and give feedback and praise. Make sure everyone who wants to, has a chance to play the child who says 'no'. Teach the children to say no in a firm voice and loudly if they need to. There are videos and curriculum listed in the back, which are designed to teach prevention skills, but this activity is a good start. The most important thing is that you give children permission to say no in your daily interactions with them.

TOUCHES AND SOCIAL DISTANCE

To create a safe environment, you need the basic understanding described in <u>Healthy and Unhealthy Touch</u> and <u>Choices Regarding Types of Touch</u>, so if you have not read those sections, please do so now. Some programs refer to 'good touch and bad touch'. Others refer to 'safe and unsafe touch'. We are using the terms 'healthy and unhealthy touch', but the important thing is that you understand the distinction and can teach children the difference between types of touch.

There are many opportunities in group settings to incorporate appropriate touch. Many games can involve hand holding. Holding hands to play a circle game is usually a 'good' touch. However, if a child doesn't want to hold hands, allow that choice.

The most important lesson here is:

Never force a child to kiss or hug someone!!

If Megan wants to hug Nathan, and Nathan doesn't want a hug, suggest a different touch option. For example, "Megan, Nathan doesn't want a hug right now. How about a high five?" We have heard many adults say things like, "Nathan, give Megan a hug so you don't hurt her feelings." We want to clearly teach children that they DO have a choice about who touches them and how. To help reinforce this, it is a good idea to develop a habit of asking permission before touching a child. For example, Susie's pony tail is drooping and you want to fix it for her, if you ask her permission first, you teach her that she has choices about who touches her.

You will notice that children are very different when it comes to touching. Some children will not initiate touches and others may seek out touching on a regular basis. You are in a unique position to observe and influence. If you have a child in the group who is frequently touching the other children and possibly invading their space, you can actively teach the child about social distance and permission for touching. Very young children can learn the 'arm's length rule' to measure if they are too close to another child. If a child has an issue with this, you can demonstrate the rule, have them practice it and give them praise for making progress. To demonstrate social distance with a group of children, make it a habit to have the children stretch their arms out between them to space the distance between them. This can seem like a game and become a fun habit within a group setting.

LANGUAGE FOR BODY PARTS

You can relax. We are not advocating that day care and preschool providers actively teach preschool children about their private body parts. We feel that this responsibility is best taught in the privacy of a family home. However, we do believe that group settings for preschool children, should provide guidance for employees on what is acceptable information to discuss with children. We believe that it is good policy to make these guidelines with the input from parents and to include these practices in new employee training. If this has not occurred, you may seek direction from your supervisor. We will provide our thoughts on this so that those readers in managerial positions have a starting point to develop some guidelines.

1. Providing Correct Information

We believe that you have a responsibility to provide accurate information when a child communicates inaccurate information. For example: A child approaches you with excitement and says, "My mommy has a baby growing in her tummy!" Your response should include factual information about where babies develop, such as, "Babies grow in their mommy's uterus. That's great! You are going to be a big sister!" Here's another example: Bobby says, "My pee pee hurts." Teacher calmly replies, "Your penis hurts? Let's go and have the nurse check it." It is always best if you use the correct term even when the child doesn't.

2. Referring To The Parent For Correct Information

Children are naturally curious and they will ask all kinds of questions. Not all information may be appropriate to discuss in a group setting. It is fine to tell a child, "That is a good question but it's private. I'll ask your mom and/or dad to talk with you about it." It is important that children learn boundaries when it comes to who to talk to about what. You can help with that. It would be helpful to make a list of topics which are referred to parents. If a parent expresses concern about speaking to their child about private matters, share this book with them.

We are recommending the development of unified terminology that can be used when communicating with children about their bodies across all settings. Parents, relatives, teachers and other caretakers are very creative at coming up with slang terms for body parts and functions to avoid saying the correct terms. Our bodies are precious gifts and there is no reason to feel ashamed about any aspect of them. The lists below might be helpful as an example of correct terms to use and terms which should be avoided

Correct term or function	Terms to Avoid
Breasts	Boobs, fried eggs, tits, melons, hooters
Penis	Talley wacker, dick, pee pee, hotdog
Vulva	Down there
Vagina	Pee pee, down there
BM (bowel movement)	Pooh, boo-boo
Urinate	Pee pee, tinkle, whiz,
Pass gas	Fart, poot

I received a call one evening from our son and was surprised when he said, "Of all the people who would teach my daughter the incorrect word for her private body parts, I never dreamed it would be you!" I was confused and asked him to explain. He went on to tell me that three year old Martha had told her parents, "I don't want breasts like Mommy. I want boobies like Grandma!"

First of all you need to understand that Martha's mother has very small breasts and I have very large breasts. When I was dressing one morning, little Martha was staying with us and happened to come into the room. She pointed at my breasts with wide eyes and said, "What's that?" I replied, "Breasts." It was obvious that the word breast did not connect with her so I said "Bosoms?" Again, there was no sign of recollection, so I said, "Boobies?" Martha responded with "Yes, boobies". Apparently she had been taught the word breasts but did not connect that word with the full-bodied figure of her grandma!

TEACHING ABOUT RELATIONSHIPS

We can teach children that not all relationships are the same. They are closest to people in their family. Families are closer physically and emotionally, especially when children are young. Families may hug and kiss but we don't hug and kiss everyone we see at the park or the grocery store. When children are at preschool or day care, they learn quickly that they don't like everyone the same and that not everyone likes them the same. They start to learn about 'best friends' and 'favorite teachers'. As children start to learn about different relationships, they learn even more about privacy and social distance and choices about types of touch. We share more private talk with people we are close to. We keep a greater social distance when we are with strangers. We choose different touch options depending on our relationship with someone. Reinforce these skills within the natural environment.

A common approach to teaching about different relationships is by using Relationship Circles. Relationship Circles can be used with a group or on an individual basis, starting with children around the age of four. Draw a large circle on a piece of paper or poster board. Then draw a small circle in the middle. The middle circle is the child and the people they live with. Now draw a circle around the middle circle. This circle represents "best friends' and 'favorite people'. Now draw a circle around that circle to represent other friends and family. The fourth circle drawn represents people the child had met and the outer circle is for strangers. Once the circles are drawn, you can talk about 'who' is in each of a child's circle. You can talk about how we treat people in each of the different circles. For example, how do we greet people in the middle circle? How do we greet people we just met? When we are sad, who do we talk to? If we need help, who can we ask to help us? For children with learning or communication difficulties, the activity can be simplified. You can reduce the number of circles and use concrete examples. Adapt the activity to the specific children in the group. (See Illustration)

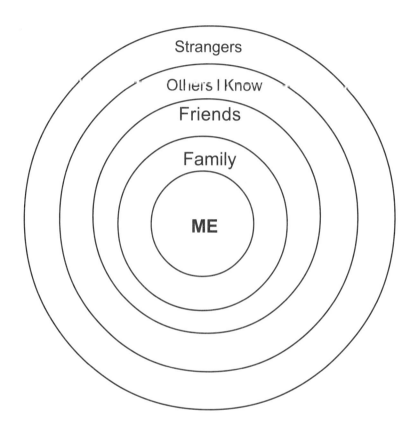

You can also read books to the children which depict various relationships. For example, there are many books about families. There are books about community helpers, such as police officers and mail carriers. Books are a wonderful way to teach and to learn! Also, the book on secrets listed in the back would be a great selection to have available for reading every few weeks.

CREATING SAFE ENVIRONMENTS IN GROUP SETTINGS - MANAGERS AND ADMINISTRATORS

As a manager or administrator of a program which provides services to preschool children and their families, you have a tremendous opportunity to create environments which can reduce the risks for sexual abuse of our young children. So far in the previous section, we have discussed the skills which can be taught and reinforced within your settings. As a manager or administrator, we hope that you encourage your employees to teach these skills and provide them with the knowledge they need to do so. Let's look at some other actions YOU can take to create safer environments!

POLICIES AND PROCEDURES

Not all group settings have policies and procedures but if your organization does, please consider adding policies and procedures on the following:

- Prohibiting abuse of any kind and the consequences;
- Privacy;
- Relationships between employees and children and their family members;
- Handling of behavioral issues which encourages learning through positive reinforcement. Focus on building positive behavior and not just reducing undesirable behavior.

Also, please review your admission and eligibility standards to see if they might exclude children with disabilities. For example, some children with disabilities may never be able to go to the bathroom independently. If your admission criteria, requires the child to be independent in toileting, some children will never be eligible. Consider instead, adaptations which could be made in conjunction with the family that would allow the child to be served.

SCREENING EMPLOYEES

As you are probably aware, people who want to sexually abuse children are going to find a way to have access to children. Some abusers are attracted to child care services to gain that access. What actions can you take to reduce the likelihood of this occurring? First of all, doing criminal background checks and reference checks on all applicants is highly recommended. These checks can be repeated periodically in case new information has become available. In your reference checks and interview process, look for signs that an applicant may have a need to control others or an attitude that devalues children, as one aspect of your screening process.

ORIENTATING AND TRAINING EMPLOYEES

As a manager or administrator, you want to give consistent messages to all employees that the safety of the children comes first and that abuse of any kind will not be tolerated. During the initial training, this message needs to be very strong with clear definitions of what is meant by abuse and clear consequences for abusive behavior. The emphasis on teaching children prevention skills should be a strong component of employee training. You should also add that parents are encouraged to drop in and visit whenever possible. Provide an in-service for employees on sexual abuse from time to time, which includes signs of sexual abuse in young children. Teaching staff not to engage in power struggles with children or their parents is another important component of employee training. If you serve children with disabilities, which we hope you do, provide any special training employees may need. Solicit help with specific training from parents.

PARENT TRAINING

Provide information to parents about your emphasis on safety and abuse prevention. This can be included in brochures or new parent orientation. Share with parents the prevention skills you are teaching. You can have an annual in-service for parents with a guest speaker on the topic. Most parents will appreciate your commitment to the safety of their children. Make sure that your employees know that the parents are well-informed. Abusers prefer to violate a child whose parents are naive.

HANDLING ALLEGATIONS

Follow up on allegations of all concerns about the care of the children. There are agencies which say they follow up on allegations but all of the employees know that 'staff can get by with just about anything". That's an agency an abuser would like to work in. You want to create a culture in which staff KNOW that you are responsive to concerns and the needs of the children and families.

EMPHASIZE EMPOWERMENT AND NOT CONTROL

Your goal is to empower children to grow and learn skills; empower staff to be creative and responsive to the children's unique needs; and empower parents to be involved and informed. That's a lot to ask, we know. When we empower children, staff will not get into power struggles with them. When we empower parents, we work together as team players to do what is best for children. When we empower staff, we reduce their frustrations and need to control the children and enhance their ownership of quality care. Empowerment includes listening to someone's ideas, respecting their opinion, involving them in decision-making, and sharing information, concerns and decisions with them, to the extent possible. When we emphasize empowerment, we are not strict about control and schedules and total compliance, but we focus on skills and abilities.

POSITIVE AND CARING INTERACTIONS

This is related to empowerment but important enough that it deserves its own section. As a parent, I want child care providers who care about my child. As professionals, we want child care providers who care about the children they work with. We know when a caretaker fails to form an attachment or a bond with a potential victim, the risk that abuse will occur is increased. Encourage your employees to care about the children and help them to find a balance if over involvement occurs. Notice if you have an employee who refers to the children as objects or treats the children less than human. For example, if an employee refers to a child as "the biter", that is cause for concern. Children should be referred to by their name, not their behavior or their disability. Pay close attention to the interactions between the employees and the children and model and reinforce individual, caring interactions. It is also important that you occasionally hear staff talking with each other. This will give you invaluable information about employee attitudes toward specific children.

We encourage you to have positive interactions with your staff and to create opportunities to celebrate successes of the children and the employees. Build in some fun activities and breaks for your employees. Elicit their input on policies, activities, and practices. We all want to feel valued and it takes all of us to raise a healthy and happy child.

SECTION 6

PARENTAL AWARENESS IN RELATION TO CARETAKERS

If you see a turtle on top of a fence,
chances are he didn't get there by himself.
Alex Haley

Parental Awareness In Relation to Caretakers

Just as you teach your child to trust her feelings about other people, you need to trust your feelings about people. This is especially true when it comes to selecting who you want to help you take care of your child. If you are uncomfortable with leaving your child with someone, trust your feelings. This can be difficult if you have a busy life. You may feel like a particular caretaker is your only option even though you are uncertain about this caretaker. Trust your feelings and ask for help. Yes, it is OK to ask for help. You might ask other parents with preschool children who they use for child care and get their recommendations. The Department of Children and Family Services in many states can provide you with information about licensed child care providers. Some states have Regional Child Care Resource Offices which can help identify caregivers. If you are receiving services from an early intervention provider, public health or social service agency, ask them to help you find some resources for child care. Seek out options until you find someone you trust.

You can also ask for a copy of the sex offender registry for your county. In some states, you can access the registry on the internet. All states have a sex offender registry but each state has their own definitions and guidelines. For example, the offenses which are included and the length of time an offender is kept on the registry may vary in different states. You can check this out by contacting the State's Attorneys Office or a local sexual assault center. You should also know that not all sex offenders are on the registry. To be on the registry, an offender must be reported, charged, and convicted of an offense which is included on the registry for that state. Some offenders are never reported and some are never convicted. Some offenders plea bargain and are convicted for a crime but not a sex crime. Some offenders are never brought to the attention of the courts. The registry includes the names and addresses of convicted sex offenders. In spite of these limitations, the registry is still a valuable tool for you to have access to.

Once you have identified a caretaker, be observant and make unexpected visits. Let the caretaker know that you will make unannounced visits and do so when you can. If your schedule makes this impossible, ask someone you know and trust to stop by unannounced. Let the caretaker know that your child's safety and well-being is your first priority. Tell the caretaker your expectations about the privacy of your child. Enlist their help in teaching your child the touch options and about private and public behavior. This alone, sends a very strong message to the caretaker. Abusers look for easy targets and they don't want to get caught.

Be observant of your child's behavior and look for signs of discomfort. If your child is verbal, ask her how her day was and listen closely to the response. It is important to note that other children can touch inappropriately. An older child at the preschool may touch inappropriately or the baby-sitter teenage son or spouse could be an abuser. Be sure and find out from the caretaker what the daily schedule and routine are and ask questions about supervision. Some sample questions might include:

- What happens if the caretaker needs something at the store?
- Does she leave her teenage son with the children while she runs to the store?
- Where do the children take their naps?
- Who provides personal assistance such as diaper changing or going to the bathroom?
- If your child has a disability and requires diaper changing beyond the age of 2, where will this occur to assure privacy?

These are important pieces of information for you to check out. It is perfectly fine to tell the caretaker, "Lots of children are abused and I am making sure it doesn't happen to mine!" A caretaker with the best interest of your child as a priority should not resist these types of precautions.

If your child attends an organized, certified day care provider, you might also want to ask the following questions:

- Who are you certifiod by?
- Can I see a copy of your last survey?
- What training do your employees receive?
- What policies and procedures do you have in place which reduce the likelihood of abuse?

A Note About Abusers

There is a myth that sexual abuse and sexual assaults occur by strangers. This is false. The majority of abusers are people who are known and trusted by the victims. Some sex offenders were sexually abused as children and have not learned proper boundaries in their own relationships. Please note that not all persons who have been abused become abusers: many become very sensitive and caring people. Abusers choose their victims carefully and 'test the waters' while developing trust with the child. The abuse doesn't usually occur at the beginning of the relationship but after the abuser has determined that this is a safe person to abuse. For the abuser this means:

- They can have access to the child when no one else will interrupt;
- The child trusts them and won't resist; and
- The child can't or won't tell anyone what has happened.

They might test the child with keeping a simple secret like giving the child candy and telling them not to tell their parents. If the child keeps this secret, the abuser might feel safe that the child will keep other, more serious secrets.

Quotes from some survivors:

"I was eleven when my uncle raped me. My mom and dad were mad at him and we don't see him anymore. I am glad."

"The bus driver did it. He got in trouble."

"My grandpa hurt me. I still see him at Christmas and at parties. Some of the family did not believe

me. My parents make sure I am never alone with him. I don't know why he hurt me like that."

"When I get mad I see him standing over my bed."

We cannot always tell who an abuser might be. Many abusers are quite charming and well-liked. We are not suggesting that you never trust anyone…what a limited life that would be for you and your family. Trust your instincts, stay in tune with your child and teach the skills we have discussed. Do what you can to reduce the chances that someone will take advantage of your child.

Dad sexually abused us girls for years and no one ever knew it. People in town loved him and I was frequently told, "I wish I had a dad as cool as yours". He would flirt with all of the teen age girls and make sexual innuendos. I hated it but I couldn't tell anyone. They all thought he was wonderful.

It is impossible to look at someone and tell that he or she might sexually abuse a child. Some sex offenders have 70 victims before they are apprehended. Some things that you can be on alert for include:

- A person who actively seeks time alone with your child or children;
- A person who seems to seek time alone with children in general;
- A person who gives your child gifts;
- A person who tells your child to keep a secret.
- A person who has questionable boundaries; breaks rules; frequent touches; etc.

If you notice these signs or if your instincts tell you to be cautious of a person, make sure your children are not alone with them. No harm is done by being cautious.

As a single parent and working mother, I rarely asked anyone to baby sit my children as I wanted to be with them when I was not working. I had to work late one night and asked my sister and her new husband to watch my children. When I arrived to pick them up, I parked the car and went inside to get them. When we got ready to leave, my car keys had mysteriously disappeared. I called someone to pick me up and take me home to get my spare car keys. My new 'brother-in-law' suggested that my children stay the night as it was getting late and they were tired. I was tired too, and very tempted after my long day but something inside told me it was a bad idea. So I went home, fetched my spare keys and took my children home to bed.

A few months later, my 'brother-in-law' was arrested for molesting his two stepdaughters. While my heart goes out to my nieces, I am forever thankful that I trusted my feelings that night and that my children were safe.

Symptoms of Abuse

Not all bad things can be prevented. No matter how hard we try, we must realize that sometimes negative things creep into our world. It is not what happens but how we deal with it that is most important. It is whether we use it as a milestone or a stepping stone. We pray that your child is never abused, but if he or she is, the sooner you discover it, the better off you and your child will be and the greater potential for recovery and prevention of further abuse.

If your gut feelings leave you with suspicion, be aware of possible symptoms of sexual abuse. In some situations, it is the symptoms which first cause the parent to be suspicious. There is usually more than one possible cause for a symptom…just like dizziness might be caused from high blood pressure, diabetes, hypoglycemia, inner ear infection or even stress. Remember that a symptom is just a sign and we need to look further.

Symptoms of possible abuse include, but are not limited to:
- Discharge from the penis or vagina*
- Bruising or swelling in the genital area*
- Blood on diaper or training pants*
- Bleeding from the rectum or vagina*
- Nervous tics, such as pulling hair plugs
- Advanced sexual knowledge for the child's age
- Advanced sexual behavior for the age of the child
- Frequent, unexplained sore throats
- Nightmares or other sleep disturbances
- Unexplained gagging
- Fear of dark or staying in room with door closed
- Extreme change in eating habits
- Bed-wetting
- Aggression
- Isolation
- Extreme change in mood, behavior or personality

- Sudden avoidance of familiar adults or places
- Avoidance of undressing or the wearing of extra layers of clothing
- Elective Mutism (can speak but elects not to speak)

(Note: The physical symptoms have the * after them.)

In small children and in children who cannot speak, physical symptoms are the most evident.

If you have the feeling that your child is being sexually abused, the police or child protective services need to be contacted. We also recommend that you consider having your child checked out by their primary care physician or local expert.

If you miss clues and later find out that your child has been abused, seek help and work through your feelings for your sake and your child's sake. We are not the ever-seeing eye. We can only do the best that we can. In this case, the best approach is to seek help through the local sexual assault center. You can call the crisis line, 24 hours a day, and you don't have to give your name or the name of your child.

In this young woman, the symptoms were physical and behavioral. A couple of years before the abuse was discovered, she began complaining of stomach pain. An ulcer was diagnosed and treated. Around the same time she became belligerent with her parents and her teachers. Behavior programs were designed and implemented with little change in her behavior. In some ways, she was lucky. She was in a class about relationships and she had a mother who listened to her. These two factors led her to tell her mother one day that her father had been touching her and making her do things that she didn't like. Her father no longer has access to her. She no longer has 'behavior problems' and her medical condition has improved.

If Abuse Occurs

If you discover that your child has been abused, or if your child tells you that she has been touched by someone, these are important factors for you to keep in mind:

1. Plan for your child's need for safety. Take steps to make sure that the person who touched your child does not have access to her. Tell your child, "I'll do my best to keep you safe".
2. Stay as calm as possible. This is going to be difficult but do what you can to stay calm for the benefit of your child. Your child needs to know that you are in control. Some children assume that their parents are mad at them if they see visible signs of anger. If your child sees you upset, you can say, "I am upset but not with you".
3. Tell your child that she did the right thing by telling you what happened. You may tell her that you are proud of her for being brave enough to tell. You can also tell her, "I believe you. I am glad you told".
4. Assure your child that she did nothing wrong. Tell her the other person was at fault. You might say, "This happens to lots of kids. Nothing you did made this happen".
5. Tell your child what you are going to do. For example, "I will keep you safe. We are going to call the police now since this person has broken the law." Keep your child informed.
6. Provide your child with opportunities to make choices. The abuser took her power away. You can help restore her sense of power by listening, understanding and giving her choices.

7. Maintain the daily routine as much as possible. There is security in having a predictable routine. Your child may cling to you for a few days after telling. This is a natural reaction and okay for you to allow.
8. Continue to reassure your child that you will protect her and help her.
9. Do not tell your child to "just forget what happened". Don't ask for details about what happened. Don't ask why she didn't tell you sooner.

If you suspect that your child has been abused, you will need to get some help. You may choose to have your child checked by a doctor, and if there are physical signs of abuse, the police will be notified. If a service provider, clergy, doctor, teacher, or child care provider suspects that your child has been abused, they are mandated by law to report this to the Department of Children and Family Services who will investigate the situation and work with the police. You might also choose to call your local sexual assault center. The employees at the center can provide you with some valuable information and the personal support you need. They are experts at the legal aspects of sexual abuse and typically provide counseling, advocacy and support. Some of these centers are not able to provide counseling for children under the age of four but can usually refer you to professional resources in the community. If your community has a Child Advocacy Center, that is another excellent resource. They work with the police and the Department of Children and Family Services in child sexual abuse investigations.

Please know that if your child is abused by a family member, it may take even more courage for her to tell someone what has happened. In this situation, you and your child may need more support to handle the emotional fall out. In some families when this happens, people take sides and hurtful comments are made. A family may be split following a sexual abuse disclosure. Stay strong and do what is best for your child. Seek out people who believe her and are supportive of you both. The bravery of children who tell on their abusers is immense.

If your child is abused, allow yourself the resources to work through the pain you will experience. You may feel physically sick, angry and guilty. These are normal reactions to a horrible violation and you are not alone. Many parents, grandparents, and extended family members have suffered similar kinds of pain and there is hope in every tragedy. By discovering the abuse early, you may have prevented years of ongoing abuse to our child. Early detection of abuse is something for which you and your child can be thankful. When the offender is a family member, the family dynamics and relationships are interrupted and often, severely damaged. Stay focused on what matters the most…the child!! There is help for recovery and strength to be gained. We have both been there and we know that this is a fact.

Abuse and Abandonment

There are many well-documented effects from childhood sexual abuse. When the abuser is someone the victim knows and trusts, there is a clear feeling of abandonment. When the abuse is not dealt with immediately, a condition is created that festers like an open cancerous wound. When a child feels abandoned and betrayed in this way, the child may also abandon their own sense of self. When there are years of sexual abuse which begin in childhood, the abandonment issues include social, physical, emotional, psychological and intellectual effects which can last a life time unless intervention occurs.

- Social effects: the fear and often the inability to have healthy interactions with self and others.
- Physical effects: the physical effects of trauma and stress; and the inability to relate or interact intimately except as a 'pay back' or a 'reward', even in a significant relationship or marriage.
- Emotional effects: the inability to commit to another on a spiritual, loving level; feeling impulsive and out of control at times.
- Psychological effects: the inability to process the cause of problems related to the abuse; feeling unworthy and unlovable.
- Intellectual effects: the inability to understand the effects of the abuse.

For a child to begin the healing process, the silence has to be broken. We are only as sick as our secrets; and often times, sexual abuse is a personal or family secret. When family members are willing to confront the issues and seek counseling and therapy, the healing process can begin. Sexual abuse validates the feeling of unworthiness; of being incapable of loving and being loved. The most important feeling in life is to feel accepted and to be loved. Sexual abuse removes this feeling from the victim and replaces it with shame. In order to regain the beauty of one's uniqueness, one must come to terms with the abuse.

Sexual abuse is a violent control issue. The offender takes control of the victim ad destroys the unique, lovable person within. Don't allow the offender to live rent-free in your brain. Seek help, break the cycle and bask in the uniqueness of your own creation. There will never be another one like you or your child. Celebrate it!

Give this heritage to your own children through education. So learn to Trust Your Children With the Information so they can bask in the beauty of their uniqueness.

SECTION 7

BEYOND PRESCHOOL YEARS

Tell your family Y.M.T.M. You Matter To Me.

Mamie McCullough

Beyond Preschool Years

As your child grows older, you will need to continue to teach the skill and make sure that you "listen" to your child. The five R's might be helpful to you in this journey of keeping your child safe:

1. Role model what you want your child to learn.
2. Remember each day that your child learns from you.
3. Repeat the lessons often. Repetition is important to learning.
4. Reinforce each skill and your child's progress along the way.
5. Reassure yourself and your child's other caregivers. Your child is worth it!

You might want to review the "10 Things I Can Do For My Child" listed in the General Information section. You are a busy person with lots of responsibilities and it is easy to forget to teach these skills. You might want to post the list on your refrigerator or place them in your bedroom where you can see them often. (We really don't care if you rip this page out.) Do whatever helps you to remember these important lessons.

As your child grows older, your influence in your child's life will be competing with many other powerful influences. By building a strong foundation, you can continue to have a positive relationship with your child as she starts school, faces puberty, begins dating and prepares for adulthood. It is important that your child knows that you are on her side. You know how much you love your child but there may be times when your child questions that.

Some parents get in a rut of negativity when their child begins to seek more independence and test the parental rules. Try and express your love an appreciation for your child, even if things are a challenge. Slip a note in your child' lunch box or a card with a note in their school book. Orieda used to put little notes on red paper hearts in all kinds of places. For example, her child might open a drawer to pull out some clothes and find a red heart with a note "folded with love". You might surprise your growing child with simple reminders that you love them. They will appreciate it…even if they don't say so. Random acts of kindness are necessary within the family. Spend time together even if that only means being in the same room sometimes. Maintaining an emotional bond with your child is the goal as they grow older. Continue to provide your child with open, honest, factual information about her body, body functions, relationships and sexuality.

Continue to teach your growing child that she has value just being who she is. If we try to change a child's hair color, walk, clothing, etc…the message is "You aren't good enough". Stay focused on what really matters…the person inside. It is hard for a girl or young woman to value her body when she looks like a Christmas tree. Many children who are in a hurry to grow up too soon, may submit to sexual activity thinking that will make them popular. When first graders know about sex baseball, and many of them do today, we have a problem. We have known many girls and women who believed that their value was between their legs. How sad. Review the "Girls and Boys" section again and think seriously about the messages you are giving your sons and daughters as they continue to grow.

As your children grow beyond the preschool years, involve them in decision-making about family matters, including money. This type of experience can teach decision-making, sharing and family cohesiveness. This is how it worked in the Anderson family. Every pay day, there would be a 'family meeting'. The parents shared how much money was available after the bills were paid. Each child would have the opportunity to express what they needed and wanted. If the children were old enough, they had to also say the approximate cost. Each member of the family had the opportunity to discuss their opinions and vote for how they thought the money should be spent. Over time, the children not only learned about money management but also learned to empathize for their siblings and to take turns in being the recipients of the family budget.

If your child has access to a personal computer, learn what you can about internet safety. There are parental controls and programs available to protect your child from sexually-explicit materials, child abductors, and solicitors of child pornography. If you are unsure where to begin, you can contact your local police department or sexual assault center. With the events that are occurring today, this is vital to protect your child from potential harm.

Many children beyond the sixth grade can learn to analyze and interpret messages from the media. Teach your child to understand what lyrics to songs mean. Help them to understand the power of words to demonstrate respect or to demonstrate disrespect. When your child hears disrespectful messages, discuss with them options for exerting their personal power to make their voice heard. For example, can your son or daughter write a letter to the radio station? Call the TV station or newsletter? Say something to a friend who may not realize the harmful effects of their comments? Awareness gives us freedom of choice. Provide your child with options from which they can choose.

When we work with very young children or with people with significant cognitive disabilities, we typically teach the four basic feelings mentioned in the section on teaching feelings. As children grow older, we can teach them a wider range of feelings which more accurately express what their experience is. It is very helpful to help children learn the feelings which are behind anger. When people express anger, it is directed outward. Usually, underneath the anger is a different feeling, such as fear or loss. It is very valuable for children to learn this as they develop emotionally. If a classmate calls your son a name, yes, he may feel angry, but what else does he feel? Is he afraid that people won't like him? Is he disappointed and sad that a friend hurt him this way? Try to help your child express these feelings. When a child learns to express his feelings using "I statements", such as "I feel sad", he is in a position to understand himself and others. **It is hard for most of us to express uncomfortable feelings.** You can help your child learn this skill from an early age. What an awesome gift you pass on when that happens.

SECTION 8

SOCIAL CHANGE

Injustice anywhere is a threat to justice everywhere.
Dr. Martin Luther King Jr.

SOCIAL CHANGE

When a child's liberty and innocence are taken, it is a terrible, terrible loss. And those responsible have committed a terrible crime. Our society has a solemn duty to shield children from exploitation and danger." President George W. Bush, White House Conference on Missing, Exploited and Runaway Children, October 2, 2002.

As a parent, teacher, or interested citizen, you might be asking yourself, "What more can I do? What can I do to make the world less dangerous for our children?" That is the focus of this section. Below are our ideas on actions that you can take to make the world safer for everyone.

Burst the bubble of implied agreement!!

That's a fancy way of saying **Speak up!**

If you hear someone say something disrespectful about women, say something!! Your silence is seen as agreeing with the statement that was made.

If you hear music being played by a certain radio station that is violent or disrespectful, call in or write a letter expressing your discomfort.

If a local court case does not make an offender accountable, express your concern.

Fight for practices and procedures which increase the number of people with disabilities who are deemed to be credible witnesses in a court of law when sexual abuse has occurred.

Encourage movie theatres to enforce R ratings for movies. Push for legislation that does not allow children to attend R rated movies with their parents.

Write a letter to the editor that supports equality among people.

If a friend or co-worker is a victim, gently offer support.

Get Involved!!

Participate in marches, programs and/or rallies to support antiviolence activities. Many communities have candlelight ceremonies for victims of violence and many sexual assault centers coordinate an annual "Take Back the Night" program to increase awareness or sexual assaults. Prevention means never having to take back the night!

Find out what prevention programs are available in your community. Encourage your child's day care, preschool, school, etc. to include prevention education as part of their services for children and families. You can check with your local sexual assault center, child advocacy center, YWCA or YMCA.

Support your local sexual assault center or child advocacy center by becoming a volunteer or donating funds. Volunteer opportunities might include clerical activities, prevention education, hot line calls and fund-raising activities.

Support legislation and funding for Healthy Families, Sexual Assault Centers and Child Advocacy Centers.

Be Informed!!

Learn more about sexual abuse prevention and treatment, legislation and research. Knowledge is power and we would love for you to be empowered to join our efforts to stop sexual abuse/assault.

The following are some resources that may help:

National Sexual Violence Resources Center
www.NSVRC.com

NSVRC provides a variety of resources on sexual violence
including links to state coalitions against sexual assault.

RAINN
Rape, Abuse, and Incest National Network
National Sexual Assault Hotline 1-800-656-HOPE
www.RAINN.com

RAINN provides statistics, counseling resources, prevention
tips, news and more.

Pennsylvania Coalition Against Rape (PCAR)
125 North Enola Drive
Enola, Pa. 17025
1-800-692-7445
www.pcar.org

PCAR has an informative newsletter called The PCAR
Pinnacle and a variety of resources. Their other websites
include:
www.menagainstsexualviolence.org
www.teenpcar.com
www.wherestheoutrage.org

Center for the Prevention of Sexual Abuse and Domestic
Violence
2400 N. 45th Street # 10
Seattle, Washington 98103
www.cpsdv.org

Provides education materials for a wide range of audiences.

Mentors in Violence Prevention (MVP) Jackson Katz, Founder
mvpstrat@aol.com
MVP Strategies
Northeastern University
716 Columbus Ave. Ste. 161 CP
Boston, Ma. 02120
www.ncasports.org/mvp

MVP provides gender violence prevention training to colleges, high schools, professional and college sports teams, community groups, corporations and the US Military. The focus is on teaching men how they can help prevent violence against girls and women. A variety of training materials are available.

Men Can Stop Rape
PO Box 57144
Washington, DC 20037-7144
1-202-265-6530
www.mencanstoprape.org

Learn how men can be involved in the movement to stop sexual violence against women.

Communities Against Violence Network (CAVNET)
www.cavnet.org

An international network of advocates and experts who deal with issues of violence and abuse. The website has many resources and documents.

National Association of Child Care Professionals
www.naccp.org

This organization serves child care owners, directors and administrators to enhance the quality of child care services. Their goal is superior child care.

National Association of Child Care Directors
PO Box 90723
Austin, Tx. 78709
1-800-537-1118

Infant-Parent Institute
www.infant-parent.com

The Infant-Parent Institute specializes in attachment problems in infancy and throughout the life span. In addition to providing clinical services, the institute has a training center and conducts research.

SECTION 8

GENERAL INFORMATION

What is a sexual assault center?

Sexual Assault Centers of Coalitions Against Sexual Assault exist in every state. Each state has a state Coalition Against Sexual Assault which manages and monitors the centers operations in that state. Sexual assault centers typically provide four functions:

1. prevention education in schools, colleges, agencies and the community to reduce the incidence of sexual violence;
2. counseling services for victims of sexual assaults;
3. advocacy services; both medical and legal for victims of sexual assaults; and
4. 24 hour hot line phone services for information and crises.

What is a Child Advocacy Center?

Child Advocacy Centers are county or multi-county programs that offer a variety of services in one facility for child victims of sexual abuse. The Centers are able to coordinate investigations among agencies and minimize the trauma for children who go through the justice system. Another function is to help investigators build stronger cases. The Center's work with law enforcement, state's attorneys offices and Child Protective Services, as well as the child and their family. While almost every state has Child Advocacy Centers, some differences can be found in state statues, funding and services.

What is Healthy Families?

Healthy Families is a program designed to assist parents before and after the birth of a new baby. The family's needs are assessed and home visits are an integral part of the services. The services include the identification of family strengths and needs, coordination of health and social services, and parent support and education. This type of early intervention can improve parent-child relationships and improve a child's chances of a healthy and safe future. To see if there is a program in your area, call 1-800-CHILDEN.

Things I Can Do For My Child

1. Love them…trust them…make a connection.
2. Encourage your child to express feelings. And remember: ALL FEELINGS ARE OKAY!
3. Listen...watch…pay attention. You know your child better than anyone.
4. Teach your child to make choices and allow her to say "no" at times.
5. Teach your child several ways to interact including hug, smile, wave, handshake, high five.
6. Let your child choose who hugs and kisses them.
7. Teach your child about their body.
8. Teach your child that some secrets need to be told.
9. Teach your child the proper space between them and another person.
10. Teach Privacy - body parts, activities, locations, talk.

APPENDIX

EDUCATIONAL RESOURCES

Books to Read With Your Children

There are many reasons to read books to your child(ren). Reading books together is a wonderful way to share information and open the door to communication. It is great fun too! Below are some books related to sexuality and keeping your child safe. We often think we can read something once or twice to our children and that our job is done. When it comes to books about sexuality, it is most often our comfort level which keeps us from reading a book again, or maybe we should say discomfort level. Some of the books below may make you uncomfortable as you read them aloud. That is okay. Begin with books you are comfortable with. Read the book alone before sharing it with your child. You may get more comfortable as you reread them. Remember that you are doing this for your child. Read the same books over and over to your child. We have included books for children of all different ages and stages.

There are many books to choose from. Go to the local library and find some you like. Here are a few suggestions.

The Berenstein Bears Learn about Strangers
By Jan and Stan Berenstein
New York: Random House, 1985.

Teaches children not to talk to strangers, not to accept gifts from strangers and not to go with strangers.

Run, Yell and Tell: A Safety Book for Children
By Carol Watson
Minneapolis: Missing Children Minnesota, 1993.

This book is about how to prevent abduction.

Proud to be Me
A Self-Esteem Coloring and Activities Book.
Flushing, NY: Promotional Slideguide, 1996.

This book teaches us how our differences make us special.

It's My Body
By Lory Freeman
Parenting Press
PO Box 75267
Seattle, Washington 98125
ISBN: 0-943990-03-3

This is an excellent book which teaches young children how to resist uncomfortable touch. It is designed for children ages 3 to 8.

Did the Sun Shine Before You Were Born?
By Sol and Judith Gordon
Amherst, New York: Prometheus Books
ISBN: 0-893-88179-1

A sex education primer in soft cover, written for ages 3 to 7. The book talks about how all families are different; includes values, lifestyles and cultures. Great book!

A BETTER SAFE THAN SORRY BOOK: A family guide for sexual assault prevention.
By Sol and Judith Gordon
Amherst, New York: Prometheus Books
ISBN: 0-87975-768-X

A soft cover family guide for sexual assault prevention for parents who have children ages 6 through 9. Beautifully illustrated.

Where Did I Come From?
By Peter Mayle
Lyle Stuart Inc. 120 Enterprise Ave. Secaucus, NJ 07094
ISBN: 0-8184-0161-3.

This book covers the differences between boys and girls; how babies are made and born; and body development. This can be read to children of any age and conveys the message, "You are special!" The great illustrations make it easy to read. It comes in paperback and hard cover.

How Was I Born?
By Lennant Nilsson and Lena Katrina Swanberg
New York: Delacorte Press. 1993.

In this book with great pictures, a big sister tells the story of the birth of her baby brother.

Ben's Secret
By Eric Dlugokinsi Ph.D. and Sandra F. Allen Ph.D.
Raleigh, NC: Feelings Factor, Inc. 1992.

Ben's Secret is a story designed to prevent sexual abuse and reduce it's destructive impact.

Good Touch. Bad Touch
An Educational Coloring and Activities Book.
Flushing, NY: Promotional Slideguide. 1996.

This book teaches about good touch and bad touch and the right to say no.

The Trouble With Secrets
By Karen Johnson

Parenting Press PO Box 75267 Seattle, Washington
98125
ISBN: 0-943990-22X

This book teaches children about the different kinds of secrets
and which secrets to tell.

About Telling
The Rhode Island Chapter of the National Committee for the
Prevention of Child Abuse.

A coloring and activity book which emphasizes 'your body is
your own' and telling a trusted adult.

AUDIO-VISUAL RESOURCES

What Ta Doo
Coronet/MTI Film and Video
St. Louis, Mo.
18 minutes
To order call: 1-800-777-8100

Program was developed for children in kindergarten and first grade. Teaches children to trust and act on their feelings; recognize lures; tell a safe person; "No-Go-Tell".

My Body Belongs to Me
Sunburst Communications
Pleasantville, N.Y.
To order call: 1-800-431-1934

Program was developed for first and second grade children. Teaches the word "private"; private body parts; good and bad touches; "No-Go-Tell".

What Ta Doo With Secrets
MTI Films and Video
St. Louis, Mo.
To order call: 1-800-777-8100

Program teaches good and bad secrets; lures; saying "No"; healing; and confiding in a safe person.

Child Sexual Abuse: A Solution
By James Stanfield Co., Inc.
To order call: 1-800-421-6534

A sexual abuse prevention program for children preschool to grade 6; includes videos for children and information for parents, teachers and administrators.

NO_GO_TELL!
By James Stanfield Co., Inc.
To order call: 1-800-421-6534

A child protection program for children with special needs ages 3 to 7. The program teaches: different relationships; private parts; okay touch and Not Okay touch; who and how to tell about abuse. Can order it with or without dolls.

Effie Dolls
By Judith Franning
To order call: 1-309-764-3048

Hand made male and female dolls are 18 inches and complete with genitals and related teaching aides. Excellent for use in teaching sex education.

CURRICULUM FOR EDUCATORS

I Can Keep My Body Safe
A Facilitator's Manual for Exercise in Sexual Abuse
Prevention
By Eric Dlugokinski Ph.D. and Sandra F. Allen Ph.D.
Feelings Factory Inc., Raleigh, NC
To order call: 1-800-858-2264

This is a body safety curriculum designed to prevent sexual abuse. The curriculum includes good and bad touches and the importance of body safety.

Reducing Vulnerability
By Marjorie Fink
Learning Publications, Inc. Holmes Beach, Florida

If the program your child attends has no abuse prevention activities or training materials, you can suggest that some be obtained and utilized. The videos, books and curriculum listed above are some that you could suggest. You can also contact your local Sexual Assault Center to arrange a presentation.

BOOKS FOR PARENTS, TEACHERS, AND SERVICE PROVIDERS

Boys and Sex
By Wardell B. Pomeroy
Dell Publishing New York, NY (991)
ISBN: 0-440-20811-4

This book was written for parents. It is 187 pages and covers puberty, young manhood, birth control and sexually-transmitted diseases.

Girls and Sex
By Wardell B. Pomeroy
Dell Publishing New York, NY

This book is for parents who want information on puberty, young womanhood, birth control and sexually-transmitted diseases. 174 pages.

Genesis: In the Beginning…Breaking the Cycle of Sexual Abuse
By Orieda Horn Anderson and Shirley Paceley
Blue Tower Training Center Decatur, IL. (2001)
To order call: toll free -1-866-258-8266

A sexual abuse prevention book for parents of preschool children with disabilities which includes: skills to teach young children to reduce their risk of sexual abuse; earl education for the development of a healthy self-esteem; signs of sexual abuse and what to do i you child is abused. Designed specifically for children with disabilities.

Just Say Know! Understanding and Reducing the Risk of Sexual Victimization of People with Developmental Disabilities.
By Dave Hingsburger
Diverse City Press, Quebec Canada (1996)
ISBN: 1896230-00-8

This is an excellent book filled with real-life stories and important messages about reducing the abuse of people with developmental disabilities. Have your Kleenex ready.

Doing What Comes Naturally? Dispelling Myths and Fallacies about Sexuality and People with Developmental Disabilities
By Orieda Horn Anderson
Hightide Press (2000)
ISBN: 1-892696-13-4

Anderson's first book challenges our beliefs and attitudes concerning the sexuality of people with developmental disabilities and provides guidance on instruction and counseling.

I Openers: Parents Ask Questions About Sexuality and Their Children with Developmental Disabilities
By Dave Hingsburger
Distributed by: Mariah Management
To order call: 1-800-856-5007

This book is written in a question and answer format. The parents ask questions and Dave answers them in an open, honest manner based on his many years of experience working with people with developmental disabilities.

BOOKS WITH MORE MATURE TOPICS FOR OLDER CHILDREN

Girls are Girls and Boys are Boys So What's the Difference?
By Sol Gordon
John Day Company New York, NY
ISBN: 0-381-99627-1.

This hardcover book covers the differences between boys and girls, puberty, how babies are made and encourages the reader to "Be Yourself".

PERIOD
By JoAnn Gardner-Loulan, Bonnie Lopez and Marcia Quackenbush
New Glide Publications, Inc.
330 Ellis St. San Francisco, Ca. 94102

This is an 89 page book about female body changes during the teen age years. It includes feelings and information about pelvic exams.

What's Happening to Me?
By Peter Mayle
Lyle Stuart Inc. Secaucus, NJ
ISBN: 0-8184-0221-0

This book discusses hormones, puberty, wet dreams, and pimples. The book has wonderful drawings.

My Body…My Choice
By Shirley Paceley and Illustrated by Annette Russo Penhallgon
Blue Tower Training Center
To Order call: 1-866-258-8266
A body safety book written for teens and adults with developmental disabilities.

AUTHORS

ORIEDA HORN ANDERSON is a private consultant who has traveled throughout the United States to provide training and consultation on human sexuality. She has been a sex educator for nearly 60 years and has worked with every conceivable population. The last 30 years she has dedicated much of her life to improving the lives of people with disabilities. She has worked in state mental health and developmental facilities, community group homes, correctional facilities and family homes. Orieda has provided employee and family training on human sexuality and has assessed and counseled countless individuals on sexuality issues. She is known for her intuitive skills, her humor and her honesty.

Orieda has two previous publications:

Doing What Comes Naturally? Dispelling Myths and Fallacies about Sexuality and People with Developmental Disabilities published by High Tide Press in 2000.

coauthored Genesis: In the Beginning…Breaking the Cycle of Sexual Abuse published by Blue Tower Training Center in 2001.

Orieda lives with her husband Howard in Moline, Illinois.

SHIRLEY PACELEY, M.A., has held a variety of positions in the human service field during the past 30 years. She is a national trainer on prevention of sexual abuse as well as a motivational speaker. Shirley is the project coordinator of a sexual abuse prevention project in Illinois for persons with developmental disabilities funded through the Illinois Violence Prevention Authority and the American Association on Mental Retardation (AAMR) 2003 Special Award recipient for her work in sexual abuse prevention.

Shirley has authored a book for teens and adults with developmental disabilities titled:

My Body...My Choice ;

coauthored Genesis: In the Beginning...Breaking the Cycle of Sexual Abuse;

produced the song Teach Me and;

 initiated the Trust the Children campaign.

Shirley is known for her passion, insight and ability to bring people together. Shirley has two adult children and lives in Decatur, Illinois.

INDEX

INDEX

A

Abandonment 34, 124
Abuse 13, 17, 18, 19, 20, 21, 22, 23, 24, 25, 29,
30, 32, 34, 39, 41, 49, 55, 62, 63, 69, 73, 74, 79, 86,
87, 93, 105, 106, 108, 113, 117, 119, 120, 121, 122,
124, 125, 129, 130, 138, 139, 143, 144, 149, 159, 164,
167, 171, 172
Abuser 56, 108, 114, 116, 117, 121, 124
Aggression 40, 89, 119
Allegations 12, 108
Allen, Sandra F. 151, 159
Assertive 73, 89
Attachment 76, 109, 139
Attitude 29, 30, 31, 33, 106

B

Babysitting 32
Behavior Problems 44
Berenstein, Jan and Stan 149
Blue Tower Training Center 163, 167, 171
Bonding 76
Boundaries 24, 66, 68, 92, 97, 116, 117
Bush, George W. President 135

C

Center for the Prevention of Sexual Abuse 137
Child Advocacy Center 13, 122, 136, 143
Child Care Centers 25
Choice 47, 48, 58, 59, 95, 131, 167, 172
Circles 63, 64, 100, 101
Classroom 86
Code 56

Communicate 30, 48, 49, 51, 58, 77
Communities Against Violence Network 138
Compliant 47, 49
compromise 77
Conceived 33
Conception 30, 33
Consenting 30
Consistent 22, 39, 69, 76, 107
Coping skills 89
Coronet/MTI Film and Video 155
Counseling 29, 34, 35, 122, 124, 137, 143, 164
Cycle 30, 85, 125, 163, 171, 172

D

Day Care 17, 32, 56, 69, 83, 86, 97, 100, 115, 136
Denial 21
Department of Children and Family Services 113, 122
Development 24, 30, 31, 32, 50, 52, 76, 98, 151, 163
Disabilities 24, 31, 45, 47, 57, 61, 63, 67, 69, 79,
84, 106, 107, 131, 163, 164, 167, 171, 172
Disclose 21, 30
Dlugokinski, Eric 159

E

Effects 19, 20, 21, 124, 131
Emergency Word 56
Empathy 77, 88
Empowered 17, 73, 76, 136
Environments 3, 17, 24, 25, 32, 81, 83, 86, 87, 103,
105
Equality 73, 77, 78, 136

F

Fault 19, 23, 121
Feelings 29, 30, 34, 35, 39, 40, 43, 44, 45, 49, 54,
56, 58, 59, 65, 67, 75, 76, 77, 78, 87, 88, 89, 95, 113,
118, 119, 120, 131, 132, 145, 151, 155, 159, 167

M

N

O

P

Other Titles Available

"Teach Me" CD - a powerful song about sexual abuse of a person with developmental disabilities. Words by Shirley Paceley, music by Jill Dixson. Useful in counseling, employee development, prevention education, parent education, and community awareness.

Genesis In The Beginning...Breaking the Cycle of Sexual Abuse, by Orieda Horn Anderson and Shirley Paceley. This book provides simple suggestions for teaching preschool children self-respect, self-esteem, and sexual abuse prevention.

My Body, My Choice, by Shirley Paceley and illustrated by Annette Russo Penhallegon. An illustrated sexual abuse prevention book for teens and adults with developmental disabilities. Can be used in individual, group or classroom settings.

Wings to Fly: Bringing Theatre Arts to Students with Special Needs, by Sally Dorothy Bailey.

Trust Children With the Information - - Poster

Doing What Comes Naturally: Dispelling the Myths and Fallacies about Sexuality and People with Developmental Disabilities, by Orieda Horn Anderson.

No! How - a video by Diverse City Press, starring persons with disabilities, on preventing abuse.

All proceeds go toward enhancing services for people with disabilities.

POSTER

Photo by: Michelle Caldwell

ORDER FORM

Name: _____

Organization: _____

Address: _____

_____
(City)   (State)   (Zip)

Telephone #: (_____) _____

Please enclose check or money order payable to:
Blue Tower Training Center P O Box 2760 Decatur, IL 62524-2760

Charge to Credit Card: _____ Visa   _____ MC   _____ Discover

CC #: _____ Exp. Date _____

_____
Name on Credit Card

Charge By Phone: 217-875-1910 ; Toll Free: 1-866-258-8266 or
Fax: 217-875-8899

TITLE	PRICE	QTY
Safe Beginnings	$19.95	_____
"Teach Me" CD	$ 6.00	_____
Genesis In the Beginning...Breaking the Cycle	$14.95	_____
My Body..My Choice	$ 7.00	_____
Wings to Fly:	$17.95	_____
Poster	$ 8.00	_____
Doing What Comes Naturally:	$19.95	_____
No! How	$30.00	_____
Subtotal	$_____	
Shipping & Handling	$_____	
Grand Total	$_____	

Shipping & Handling: $0 - $20   add $3.95
                        $21 - $50   add $4.95
                        $51 - $100   add $5.95
                        $101 & Over   Please Call